Children of the Sun

22MAY93

To Jody, my beloved
wife who continuously
seeks to diversify her
perspectives and broaden her
children's literature interests.
Love
Guirlaine

Children of the Sun

Selected Writers and Themes in South African Children's Literature

ELWYN JENKINS

Ravan Press   Johannesburg

First published by Ravan Press
PO Box 31134 Braamfontein 2017
South Africa

First published 1993

Cover illustration Anno Berry
Cover design Ingrid Obery, Ravan Press
Index compiled by Sharon Rubin

ISBN 0 86975 438 6

The financial assistance of the Centre for Science Development (HSRC, RSA) towards the publication of this work is hereby acknowledged. Opinions expressed in this publication and conclusions arrived at, are those of the author and are not necessarily to be attributed to the Centre for Science Development.

Printed by Sigma Press

ACKNOWLEDGEMENTS

I acknowledge with thanks those people and institutions who have made this book possible. Vista University gave me sabbatical leave and a research grant; the South African Teachers' Association awarded me the Centennial Education Grant; members of the staffs of ISKEMUS (Inligtingsentrum vir Kinder- en Jeuglektuur en -Media of the University of Stellenbosch), the Transvaal Education Media Service, the Vista University Library and the State Library willingly gave professional assistance; Jay Heale gave advice and inspiration; David Lewis-Williams kindly read and commented on the draft; and the editors of the following publications in which earlier versions of some of the chapters appeared kindly gave permission to republish:
* Chapter One first appeared in *Oral Tradition and Education*, conference proceedings edited by Edgard Sienaert and Nigel Bell, Durban: Oral Documentation and Research Centre, University of Natal, 1988.
* Chapter Two first appeared in *Oral Tradition and Literacy*, conference proceedings edited by Richard Whitaker and Edgard Sienaert, Durban: Oral Documentation and Research Centre, University of Natal, 1986.
* Chapter Three first appeared in *Reality*, September 1989.
The views expressed here are entirely my own.

Let me find sweet roots and honey,
Let me come upon a pool.

San prayer
(Adapted by Arthur Markowitz)

CONTENTS

Introduction

The history of South African children's books written in English mirrors the interaction of South Africa's peoples, and their relationship with the land. The curiosity and romance which brought early travellers to this country and which transfuse the records of their travels were later transferred to the books written by South Africans for local children. Curiosity led to some of the very first local books being versions of the folktales of the indigenous inhabitants; romance soon turned to nostalgia for a time when wildlife was abundant and adventurers wandered free across an 'unspoilt' land. By the end of the nineteenth century times had changed: the wilderness had been tamed, and black people had become a labour resource. The twentieth century has seen many more changes, with a dramatic increase in the rate of change in the final twenty-five years – an increase matched by an upsurge in the publication of children's books.

Not many children's books in English have been published in South Africa; it is only in the last quarter of the twentieth century that the numbers have risen from perhaps a dozen in a year to about a hundred. Those that have eventually achieved publication have been staunchly South African in setting and theme, turning again and again to the cultures and history of its peoples, and the landscapes, flora and fauna of the country.

The writers of South African children's books at the end of the twentieth century continue the tradition of creating a South African literature. Not only do they retell the folktales of the black people;

1

they write new stories in imitation of them; they merge black beliefs and myth with the concerns of modern white children in stories of fantasy; they shift in historical fiction from the Eurocentred history of school syllabuses in order to explore other perspectives; they show black and white teenagers of today at the very first painful stages of getting to know and understand each other; they write about conservation and give animals the power of speech so that children can begin to understand the natural world in which they live. And it is no longer only whites who write in English: decades after the first English prose and verse by black writers was published, stories written in English by black writers about black children are beginning to appear, bringing authenticity to their portrayals which whites, no matter how well-meaning, have not been able to achieve.

Ideologies and attitudes have changed, and children's books reflect this. Black writers are now publishing their own English versions of African folktales; and the retelling of African folktales by whites is no longer motivated by curiosity about the alien, or social Darwinist ideas about the childishness of 'primitive' cultures, or nostalgia for a childhood spent listening to tales told by the old ones; today it is a celebration of the richness of other cultures, a recognition of the other person. Behind the retelling, and behind the historical fiction, lies a desire to confess and make reparation for what colonialism did to the indigenous people. Stories of teenagers caught up in the events of social and political change since 1976 show a willingness to explore new paradigms of human relations in South Africa. Modern stories told in emulation of African and San oral literature, and fantasies in which humans, animals and mythological beings collaborate to combat evil forces threatening the ecology of land and oceans, acknowledge that there are other ways of knowing Africa besides the reductionist, anthropocentric way of the whites. In these stories, animals are ennobled because of the guilty realisation that humans have ravaged the environment. A spate of children's books and youth novels has appeared, celebrating the beauty and wonder of the country and stressing humankind's physical and spiritual dependence on nature. Children's fiction set in the African bush has always been didactic, but whereas until the time of *Jock of the Bushveld* the lessons to be learnt were either scientific facts or the values of manliness, loyalty and fair play that were given scope by

2

the brutal interaction of man and nature, today the lessons are about the moral and pragmatic obligation of humans to conserve the environment.

This book presents case studies of these trends, but it would not be enough to attempt to trace only an 'African' element, for the children's books and youth fiction published in South Africa are shaped by many influences. Writers of children's books in English in South Africa write within a vast tradition and a contemporary context, both of which shape in a multitude of ways the sort of book that is eventually published. All of them are heirs to the tradition and conventions of European children's books; Marguerite Poland and Jenny Seed, for example, openly acknowledge this influence. The novels for young teenagers which have become popular in recent years must be seen in the context of modern trends in this field overseas – especially in Britain, the USA and Australia. Even when the authors themselves may not be too familiar with their overseas and South African contemporaries (to their detriment – which is obvious at times), their readers are likely to be, and so are reviewers and critics; and the comparative standards that may consequently be applied can be enlightening in evaluating the local works. Although very little criticism of children's books is published locally except in the form of scattered reviews, a substantial body of criticism has developed overseas which provides norms of quality for such genres as folktales, animal stories, picture books, historical fiction, fantasy, and teenage 'problem' novels.

South African children's books in English are also part of the much larger South African literary scene, which includes children's fiction in other languages (especially Afrikaans), the written-to-order books of the education departments, and adult fiction and non-fiction. There is no sharp division between children's books in English and in other South African languages because so much is published in translation as well. Differences in approach between English- and Afrikaans-speaking writers can be distinguished throughout the history of children's books in South Africa up to the present, but the mutual influence has been strong. For that reason this study, while not pretending to investigate the full range of English and Afrikaans books, does include some Afrikaans ones for comparative purposes.

There are also significant links between adult books and children's books. Since the 1970s a considerable amount of literary criticism has been published which analyses in detail the history of South African English literature. Although this criticism totally ignores children's literature, its account of adult literature as a manifestation of social history casts light on similar trends in children's books. In fact, this criticism is the poorer for its ignorance of children's literature. For example, prominent critics claim that white writers have never come to grips with Africa, and they keep on calling for a merging of the African past with the white present, and for white writers to face the challenge, in the words of Jeremy Cronin,

To learn how to speak
With the voices of the land.[1]

South African children's writers have, in fact, grappled with this since early in the twentieth century, and they have come a long way towards artistic solutions to this challenge.

Children's books can also be placed in the context of the social history of the country, and this can be as enlightening as placing them against adult literature. Both contexts illuminate the choice of plots and themes, and the attitudes, assumptions and perceptions of the authors. They also draw attention to significant aspects of the books that might have been overlooked.

Two agencies have particularly influenced children's books – not only their contents, but their physical appearance and, in fact, their very existence. These agencies are the publishing trade and the education departments. One of the reasons why so few children's books in English have been published in South Africa is that local publishers were unwilling to accept them. Presumably their reason was that they were too much of a risk because of the small local market. Ironically, the same argument could not be used for the equally tiny Afrikaans market, or no Afrikaans books would ever have been published. Language loyalty must have overcome financial arguments to allow so many fine Afrikaans children's books to see the light of day. The large increase in Englishlanguage children's books in the 1980s is due in no small degree to the encouragement given to English authors by Afrikaans publishing houses with a well-established history of children's book publishing. Latterly, publishers' creation of awards

4

for manuscripts has elicited some of the best new books to be published. Another new development is the creation of black publishing houses which, while encouraging black authors, do publish in English. On the negative side, the domination of the scene by Afrikaans publishers has resulted in books which are written in, or translated into, poor English, and are in other ways of poor quality by international standards. Matters of translation, illustrations and format, and, of course, whether a book is to be published at all, are kept firmly out of the hands of authors. In recent years, for example, the proliferation of translations (sometimes resulting in the simultaneous release of a book in five or six languages) can be put down to economic exigencies. Incredibly, African folktales are even being translated back into African languages for the school market.

The economics of book publishing and the effect that this has on standards ties up closely with the influence of government education departments on children's books. Because the ordinary retail market is so small, having books prescribed for use in schools offers a most attractive financial return, particularly in black schools where the numbers are so large. The industry that has developed to meet this demand is not conducive to quality. If, in the education departments for whites, a novel or volume of short stories is prescribed for the Senior Certificate or recommended for reading in junior classes, this makes the difference between a print run of hundreds and one of tens of thousands. The extremely cautious selection policies of the departments for both Afrikaans and English books have meant that very few South African books with post-World War II themes have been approved. Similar conservatism has ensured that these books are not even approved for school libraries, nor are they to be found in certain public libraries, with the result that the potential book-buying public (estimated at between two and five per cent of the population) does not become familiar with the range of contemporary children's books that are published. Children's books on modern social themes have also been subjected to the ultimate sanction of being banned by the government.

In spite of the economic and political constraints on children's books publishing in South Africa, a literature has been created that deserves to be better known and appreciated. However, I believe that we are not yet ready for a critical history – a complete survey

5

– of South African children's literature in English, for we have too few critical signposts. What little criticism there is consists of short articles, reviews or conference papers. In this book I take a few genres and authors to see whether we can begin to identify what is important and good; to understand why the books came to be written and what they tell us about South African society. The detail required for this uncharted exploration does not leave space for a comprehensive survey that would trace the development of all the genres of children's literature – not only fiction but also poetry, drama, picture books and non-fiction – for children from the very young to young adults.

In making this selection I have already exercised critical judgement: I have selected those genres, themes and authors that I believe are important, and, in some cases, I have had to decide which books best illustrate the conclusions to which I have come. I have concentrated on works published in the twenty-five years up to 1990, since I wish this book to reflect modern literature, and works published earlier are markedly different and of more historical interest than relevance to the modern reader.

The topic for Chapter One is folktales in translation, which constitute the largest identifiable genre of South African English children's books. Because of the large number of such books, I have selected a few, mostly recent, examples that best illustrate my argument. Two of South Africa's most important children's authors form the subjects of Chapters Two and Five: Marguerite Poland for her pre-eminent critical status, and Jenny Seed as one of our most prolific and also consistently good writers. In the case of Poland, I have chosen to discuss all her animal stories, and in the case of Seed I discuss all her historical novels.

The other chapters explore what I believe are the major themes in the literature. Chapter Three is the only historical study, investigating the shift to South African subject matter that occurred in English teaching at the end of World War II, and the local, or 'Bushveld', literature that became popular at the same time. In particular, I identify one key text, Victor Pohl's *Bushveld Adventures*. The Bushveld books of that time were the precursors of modern fiction that deals with one of today's most popular themes, the conservation of the natural environment. In Chapter Four I take all the works of fiction on the subject published in the ten years up to 1990 and analyse them individually, since each is so different that a generalised discussion would not bring out the variety of issues that they raise. Finally, in Chapter Six, I consider what I believe to be the most dramatic theme in modern South African English children's literature, that of race and social issues, and refer to most of the relevant fiction published in the last decade.

No doubt some important books and authors have fallen through the net. But for readers seeking guidance, this work has the advantage that most of the books discussed in detail are still in print. I invite the reader to embark with me on a reading in which, in the words of the San prayer, we may find sweet roots and honey, and occasionally, in this harsh African climate, come upon a pool.

NOTES

1. The poem 'To learn how to speak' by Jeremy Cronin (1983) is quoted by Michael Chapman in a broadcast talk published as 'A sense of identity', *CRUX*, 24:1, February 1990, 44, and by Malvern van Wyk Smith, *Grounds of Contest*, Cape Town: Juta, 1990, as an epigraph.

CHAPTER ONE

Folktales in Translation

W hat began as observational notes in the journals of early travellers soon became a genre of published literature in its own right: the oral tradition of the inhabitants of South Africa as transcribed and translated by travellers, missionaries, ethnographers, government officials, professional writers, and ordinary people who love the stories and wish to share them with others. The pattern of publishing, which continues with increasing momentum to this day, was set by two books published four years apart in the 1860s, *Reynard the Fox in South Africa, or, Hottentot Fables and Tales*, by W.H.I. Bleek (1864) and *Nursery Tales, Traditions and Histories of the Zulus, in their own Words, with a Translation into English, and Notes*, by Bishop Henry Callaway (1868).

By the early twentieth century versions of folktales were being published specifically for children, notable examples being *Outa Karel's Stories: South African Folklore Tales* by Sanni Metelerkamp (1914) and *How the Ostrich got his Name and Other South African Stories for Children* by Annette Joelson (1926), and by 1990 at least 150 different books of folktales had been published in English, three-fifths of them since 1965. At the same time Afrikaans writers have produced many Afrikaans children's books containing translations of folktales from the original languages, pioneered by the influential G.R. von Wielligh with his *Boesman-*

stories: Mitologie en Legenden in 1919. I do not say that the Afrikaans development *paralleled* the English one, for that would imply that the two had developed separately, whereas there has been such an interchange between them by way of translation that they are part of a single tradition of children's literature in South Africa.

Folktales from many South African sources have been translated and published. In addition to those of the San, Khoekhoen and Bantu-speaking peoples, I.D. du Plessis instituted the recording of Cape Malay folktales with his *Uit die Slamse Buurt* in 1939, followed by many other volumes. His stories were translated into English, and were retold yet again in a new version in 1989 by Valerie Stillwell in *Monsters, Heroes and Sultans' Daughters: Cape Malay Folktales Retold*. Only one story from Dutch/Afrikaans folklore has been translated into English in the form of a children's book, *Van Hunks and his Pipe* by Leon Rousseau, but more Dutch/Afrikaans folklore, as well as modern myths in English and Afrikaans, has appeared in books for adults such as *They Walk by Night* by Eric Rosenthal, *Myths and Legends of Southern Africa* by Penny Miller, and *The Rabbit in the Thorn Tree: Modern Myths and Urban Legends of South Africa* by Arthur Goldstuck.

Collections of African folklore published in South Africa also often include folktales from other parts of Africa, in particular Zimbabwe, from where some of the writers also come. In fact, the little country of Rhodesia, later Zimbabwe, has, like South Africa, produced a disproportionate number of books of folktales in translation. This possibly reflects the strong ethnographic tradition among Zimbabwean whites as evidenced by their famous journal, *NADA (The Southern Rhodesia Native Affairs Department Annual*, which ran from 1923 to 1980). So intrinsic a part of South African children's literature have translated folktales become that writers are now producing new, original stories in the style of San and African models. Examples of books by prominent writers who have entered this field are Marguerite Poland's *The Wood-ash Stars*, Jenny Seed's *Khulumi the Brave* and Cicely van Straten's *The Great Snake of Kalungu and Other Stories*. Poland's use of these models is examined in the next chapter.

Folktales in translation form a considerable proportion of the limited number of children's books published in South Africa, and within the super-heated racial sensibilities of the country this

9

cross-cultural enterprise is obviously a significant phenomenon. Why are these books published? What are they like? What is their ideological significance? In this chapter I consider some of the books, especially those published since 1965, in order to answer these questions.

The economics of publishing folktales

Obviously, books of folktales in translation are commercial enterprises – in fact, the earliest translations were published by missionaries largely as fund-raising endeavours. The upsurge of publishing in this field in recent years indicates that it is meeting a public demand which is possibly rooted in the dismantling of apartheid and the consequent desire of whites to learn more about African culture, as well as an assertion by black people of their own culture. As is usual with children's books, sales are to a large extent dependent upon the selection by *adults* of what they believe will be either good for children or what children should (rather than do) enjoy, so trends in the market reflect adult concerns more than children's tastes. Publishers also exploit the ambiguity over whether the books are for child or adult readers, even though the format and style may be obviously aimed at children: four recent books, for example, proclaim on their back covers that they are for 'readers of all ages' (*Monsters, Heroes and Sultans' Daughters* by Valerie Stillwell), 'young and old alike' (*The Snake with Seven Heads* by Gcina Mhlope), 'children of all age groups' (*Xhosa Fireside Tales* by Nombulelo Makhupula), and 'adults as well as children' (*The Best of African Folklore* by Phyllis Savory).

Another market opening up is that of the potentially vast black readership, which creates a demand for books in the vernaculars as well as in English. To meet it, publishers such as those of Geraldine Elliot, Rosalie Liguori-Reynolds and Hanneke du Preez shrewdly publish their books in translations into many languages (with an eye on the school trade), while black publishing houses recently began publishing folktales retold in English by black writers, presumably for both black and white readers.

That the retelling of folktales has become an industry is indicated by two kinds of *recycling* of tales: retelling of stories already collected by someone else, and republishing one's own stories, sometimes reworked, in new collections. The extent of the former

10

is difficult to assess, since the tales are public property and the retellers do not always indicate their sources, but it is certainly very common. In the latter category Afrikaans writers republish more frequently than English, but Phyllis Savory is an obvious English example. Besides all the book publishing and republishing, the material is made to stretch even further by conversion into gramophone records – Hugh Tracey, for example, made a series including *The Lion on the Path*.

Folktales as anthropology

Because all but the most recent books were intended for white readers, and hence for a culture different to that from which the stories came (a fact which is usually prominently announced on the cover or title page), the writers are tempted to meet the curiosity of whites, or even to instil curiosity where it did not exist before, by taking a slightly pedantic or anthropological stance. In fact, it is sometimes difficult to decide whether a collection of tales has been published for an anthropological purpose or to entertain children.

For example, I consider that Baumbach and Marivate's *Xironga Folk-tales*, which was published in a series by the University of South Africa's Department of African Languages 'to save some of the beautiful Varonga folklore from extinction', is an academic project, but Emma Bedford includes it in an article on 'Illustrated children's books in South Africa', where she criticises its illustrations as being 'so dramatically stylised that one wonders whether children will perceive these as illustrations or merely as decorative designs'.[1]

Phyllis Savory, who has published tales from various peoples, falls back on an anthropological rationale when she is not recounting tales recalled from her own childhood among the Matabele. Her introduction to her Xhosa tales in *African Fireside Tales Part 1* reads like a bad primary school text book:

The land inhabited by the Ama-Xhosa clans occupied the area of roughly 27 to 29 degrees East latitude, by 32 degrees to 34 degrees South latitude ... The name of the earliest known ancestor of these people was of the tribal

11

> *name of M-'Nguni ... Coming as they did from the North*
> *East of Central Africa, many of the characteristics of the*
> *Xhosa people are shared with the East African people.*
> *This can be traced in the Folk Tales. (11)*

Her dubious lesson continues with tracing the links of the Xhosa to the ancient Egyptians, Arabs, Hamites and Hebrews. The sepia illustrations to this section, by Gerard Bhengu, add to the school-room atmosphere with their old-fashioned formality. Ethnographic interest is also the reason she gives for retelling the Batswana tales: 'These variations – and there are many of them – are to be found thousands of miles apart ,,, This significant fact, and the deep interest of the particular tales, has decided me to retell them ...' (172). Her publisher's blurb also stresses her contribution to preserving folktales.

Whereas the white publishers promote the otherness of the tales (Madeline Murgatroyd's is typical in emphasising that those in *Tales from the Kraals* 'have as their background the remote re-gions of Zululand' [dust jacket]), black publishers and writers evince pride in their own black culture, coupled with a sense of urgency about the need to preserve it. The notes on the back of Makhuphula's *Xhosa Fireside Tales*, published by Seriti sa Sech-aba Publishers, remark that 'it is sad that in modern times there seems little time to sit down and tell tales as our ancestors did,' and Leshoai converts this regret into respectable ethnographic terms in his Foreword to *Iso le Nkhono: African Folktales for Children*: 'It has become quite a common practice for African scholars to collect and record the oral traditions of their various nations' (1). To varying degrees the authors take the anthropologi-cal approach further by extending their critical apparatus beyond an introduction. Savory has short 'authoritative' forewords by emi-nent figures such as Sir Robert Tredgold and Sir Seretse Khama; Murgatroyd includes a glossary suitable for even young children to use, and Diana Pitcher gives a simple pronunciation guide in *The Calabash Child*. Savory also gives a few glossarial footnotes and formally records the names of the informants for her Batswana tales.

In addition to writers' stressing the importance of collecting and accurately preserving the tales, some books are actually shaped by ethnographic enterprise. Jenny Seed's *The Bushman's*

Dream, Diana Pitcher's books, Phyllis Savory's *The Little Wise One* and Jack Cope's *Tales of the Trickster Boy* are factitious cycles of tales taken from various sources and unified. Jenny Seed shows the enthusiasm of an amateur anthropologist. In her Author's Note she recalls her delight when she came across the San stories collected by Bleek and Lloyd, and how she then set about reshaping them:

> Like the pieces of pottery an archaeologist might find in
> some ancient midden, none of the tales seemed by them-
> selves complete, but joined together they made a meaning-
> ful shape – a shape which, I feel, is not very different from
> that which the Bushmen themselves intended. (7)

The cultural arrogance of what she was doing in imposing Western concepts on the material escaped her: 'It seemed to me that they were, in fact, the story of the Creation, Bushman style' (7).

For *The Calabash Child* Pitcher creates a group of characters, who then are the actors or narrators in a series of stories roughly following the human life cycle. To make the cycle, she draws on an eclectic range of stories from southern, central, east and west Africa. There is, of course, nothing authentic about such 'cycles'. Ruth Finnegan points out in her standard study, *Oral Literature in Africa,* that this is a peculiarly Western approach. Even the gathering together of stories about a single character 'may represent the outlook of the Western systematising scholar rather than the intentions of the narrators'.[2] In *The Mischief Maker* Pitcher unifies stories about the trickster hare by giving him one name, 'Nogwaja'. Cope, following the pioneering attempt at ethnography of Bishop Callaway (whose stories he is using), links together in a serial narrative stories of the Zulu trickster, Hlakanyana, and gives his book further unity by creating a narrator figure, Mamethu, and her audience of children. Savory follows her usual ethnographic method by arranging her collection of stories of the trickster hare by country of origin.

Coupled with the sense of the remoteness of the stories in time and place is the nostalgia that some writers feel for their rural childhood, when they first heard the stories. Leshoai dedicates his book to his grandmother and parents and says 'an attempt has ... been made to keep [the stories] as they were told originally' (2).

Similarly, Makhuphula dedicates hers to 'my grand- mother, Nokulila, source of my inspiration'. Savory places the Matabele stories in the context in which she originally heard them. For example, she introduces a story by recounting,

> *We [she and her childhood companion, Farewell] climbed up on to the wagon as it bumped over the mealie stubble, and begged to be told about Vundla, Mvuu and Chipembere. I think that Chakuti was sorry for us in the loss of our pet, for he commenced straight away.*
> (African Fireside Tales Part 1 *110)*

The authors and their publishers suggest that it is their intention to compensate today's children for experiencing a childhood that is deprived of the 'paradise' (*African Fireside Tales Part 1* 108) that the authors enjoyed.

The appeal of the stories

The authors, their patrons and their publishers come up with three reasons why the stories should appeal to modern children: didactic value, intrinsic value and sheer entertainment. Sir Robert Tredgold suggests, 'The small people of Zimbabwe, and elsewhere, will find them vastly entertaining and full of knowledge of nature' (*African Fireside Tales Part 1* 105), and Madeline Murgatroyd's publisher also emphasises the attraction of the natural setting, 'where the African children are in close contact with birds, plants and animals' (*Tales from the Kraals* [dust jacket]). In practice, of course, the modern reader will not learn much about nature from the stories that is scientific in the Western sense, as most of the nature stories are about talking animals, with trickster or aetiological themes.

A new didacticism with a distinctly 1980s flavour is that of Nick Greaves's book, *When Hippo was Hairy*, which is unique in supplementing the African and San folktales with sections of scientific information about the animals featuring in the stories. The aim of the book is avowedly to promote conservation. The stories, Greaves believes, are an indictment of humans. Animals were created first, according to the San story with which he opens the book:

Last of all came man. By then, there was only one role left in the great scheme of things, so the Creator and Mantis assigned this place to the Bushman – that of Hunter-Gatherer. The Bushman fulfilled his designated role faithfully, living in close harmony with the animals, birds and the plants upon the earth ... According to Swazi folklore, animals all lived together in peace before the coming of man, and only when he finally appeared did predation, or meat-eating, spread through the world. Man preyed upon beast; beasts then preyed upon their former friends – even the reptiles and birds copied the deadly example of man. With the coming of man into the world, so fear was born. (14)

In contrast to the stories, the scientific information that he provides is starkly Gradgrindian, like something out of a children's encyclopaedia or Bitzer's definition of a horse in *Hard Times*: 'Species: Wild Dog (*Lycaon pictus*). Gregarious, found in large packs of up to 30' (39). Although other modern writers and publishers of folktales are not as explicit as Greaves about the themes of primordial harmony, the exemplary symbiosis of hunter-gatherers and nature, and modern awareness of the need for conservation, a belief in the metaphysical value of the stories in our conservation-conscious era may well underlie both the publication of so many books of folktales today and their appeal to readers.

A different didactic argument is that 'African folklore is rich in wisdom' (*The Calabash Child* cover), an argument which Leshoai takes seriously:

The choice of these legends, folk-tales and stories has been influenced by the sociological and political life of the people of South Africa. After all, in traditional African life, they serve as conscience prickers and also to educate and entertain children and adults alike. It is hoped that the readers will enjoy the collection with this in mind.
(Iso le Nkhono 2)

Yet in spite of what he avers, white readers (adults, let alone children) will find the stories in his collection so alien and enigmatic that they are most unlikely to see in them any political or moral relevance. However, the hope that these stories can be used to teach white children something about black culture is understandable. White children are heirs to a European and American literary culture that excludes anything African, and it can be argued that they are disadvantaged by this cultural gap. Professor Herbert Vilakazi said in 1987 that

> *the crisis was not with black education but with white education. Whites had been cut off from a full education and the reality of their country by being insulated from black thinking, culture, folklore, philosophy and spiritual wealth.*[3]

Less ambitious reasons for the appeal of the stories are the rather lame claims that they have 'much beauty and interest' (Sir Seretse Khama), 'deep interest' (Savory) (in *African Fireside Tales Part 1* 169 and 172) and so on. It is questionable whether the academic interest of the stories would appeal to children, and as for the beauty of the stories, that would depend on what has been selected: the dreadful stories of cannibals, ogres, monsters and cruel treatment of women and children to be found in some collections (especially Leshoai's) are likely to repel young white readers.

On safer grounds are those authors who keep their avowed intent to entertain their audience, by selecting only stories which they believe will indeed appeal to modern children, and by concentrating on a written style which will attract and engross their young audience. Animal stories – about tricksters or with aetiological themes – seem to be the favourites for sheer entertainment. Pitcher, Savory and Cope have produced cycles about tricksters, and Lesley Whitwell has written three light-hearted little books, each of which contains only one story – two about tricksters and one on how certain animals acquired their colours (*Sungura's Tug of War*, *The Stolen Mealies* and *Tortoise's Magic*). Other collections usually include stories of this kind, which children of any culture should find humorous. Hugh Tracey says in his Foreword to *The Lion on the Path and Other African Stories*,

> *Humour, conscious and unconscious, is dominant in a large proportion of the stories I have heard. It would take an expert to define the typical quality of the African sense*

16

of fun, though, like that of the British, it may often be described as a keen appreciation of the discomfort of others. (xi)

The stories he tells are full of humour, not always at the expense of someone else. The funniest is 'The girl and the crocodile', in which a girl takes a crocodile to a party, where he disgraces himself by getting drunk and singing loudly. The girl is taught the unlikely lesson that she should never invite a crocodile to a party.

Even when gruesome or sad stories are told, the manner of narration makes the difference. Some books make an immediate impression with a lively, personal style, plenty of dialogue and a sensible use of modern, colloquial English. In *Tales from the Kraals* Murgatroyd, whose stories are mainly aetiological, presents herself unambiguously as the narrator to a specific audience: 'I do believe … ' (21); 'You may be sure … ' (31); 'He put his hand out eagerly, and – (I told you magic was aiding him) – a handful of gorgeous colour was his' (20). She engages the audience with questions: 'I am sure you have often popped the leaves into your mouth. They are so lovely and sour-sweet, aren't they?' (55).

An alternative is to create a narrator figure, who can give the individual flavour of a 'character' to the narration. This was the device employed by Sanni Metelerkamp in 1914. Her narrator's language took on the flavour of the period: her Outa Karel spoke in a Cape Dutch/English children's patois that sounds rather like the 'precious' language of the children in Pauline Smith's *Platkops Children* of the same period. Many subsequent writers have followed this technique of using a narrator, though not all have exploited its stylistic potential.

Dialogue is not used as much as it could be. Geraldine Elliot's popular *The Long Grass Whispers* of 1939 was written largely in dialogue form. Many modern writers introduce it only a snatch at a time, although Valerie Stillwell and Elsa Joubert (*The Four Friends and Other Tales from Africa*) use a lot of dialogue. However, it is rare to find the action carried forward by dialogue, as in this instance:

One man said: 'Look at those fat pigeons. I will kill them and give them to the children to make soup for their sick mother.'

17

*'No, no,' cooed the two white birds. 'You must not kill
us. Leave us alone for we have work to do here.'*

*The people stood back. Talking birds! Strange things do
our ears hear on this day!*

'Who are you?' they cried.

*'We are the spirits of the ancestors of those who live in
this hut,' they replied. 'We know someone in there is in
serious trouble.'*

*'Your words are indeed true,' said the man who, a few
minutes before, had wanted to kill the pigeons. 'Khoko's
wife cannot speak, eat or drink. A wooden spoon belonging
to her husband is stuck fast in her throat. We have tried in
vain to help her'*

'Is her husband here?' asked the pigeons.

*'No, his place is empty,' the man replied. 'He left many
days ago to go beer-drinking somewhere across the river.
He has not been seen since.'*

*'We will look for him and send him straight home,' said
the two pigeons.*

(Khoko the Lazy by Rosalie Liguori-Reynolds)

The language of this conversation exemplifies a stylistic weakness
in many of the books under consideration, in that it fluctuates between modern colloquial English (the banal 'in serious trouble')
and a pseudo-archaic 'storytelling' style (the inversion and unnecessary modal of 'Strange things do our ears hear on this day').
Writers love to sound old-fashioned. Madeline Murgatroyd, in
Maduma, Teller of Tales, which was published in 1987, still used
the obsolete spelling *kopje*. (She was 85 when it was published
and she died, much venerated, three years later – but her publisher
should have updated it.) Even the liveliest and most 'modern'
book, Whitwell's *Sungura's Tug of War*, moves from the racy style
of 'He shot up the bank and yelled "Pull" at the top of his voice',
to the stilted formality of ' "Greetings, brother!" "A good day to
you, little one" '. Savory's *The Best of African Folklore* has a less
archaic style than her earlier works, but the remnants of the old
style are ill-matched with modern colloquialisms and clichés such
as 'mighty scared' (5) and 'incredibly beautiful' (10).

There is something to be said for the appeal that lies in both
approaches to retelling these stories: the traditional opening and

closing formulae and quaint diction link them with the fairy tales of other cultures, but on the other hand modern children are more likely to be attracted by a style carefully composed for their enjoyment, such as Pitcher achieves:

> *His shoulders itched. Something rubbed his ankles, his knees. His ears twitched. Hyena quivered all over. This was terrible. He rolled over and over on the grass to try to scratch his back; he rubbed his ears against the tree trunk; he licked his elbows and ankles. It was no use; his skin felt as if it were full of coarse sand and the itching became worse.*
>
> *Hyena rushed back to where he had last heard Hare.*
>
> *'Hare, help me, help me. I am going mad with the itch,' he barked, piteously.*
>
> *Hare was sitting beside the dying embers. He sniffed as Hyena approached.*
>
> *'Hyena,' he said, 'you smell like stale dung. Please do not come near me. You are putting me off my dinner.' Taking some roast corn from the embers Hare loped off across the plains and disappeared.*
>
> (The Calabash Child 7)

Quite the liveliest, most zestful stylist is Hugh Tracey. It takes a quotation of only four lines to convey his incomparable manner:

> *When he lifted his paw, there, underneath, was a rabbit. Flat.*
>
> *'Well ...' said Lion, 'It is a pity to waste a good rabbit.'*
>
> *So he ate him all up.*
>
> (The Lion on the Path 30)

There are many other authors who are not really conscious of making a choice about style. They simply bumble along.

The appeal of the books can also be judged from their design. In 1946, Jessie Hertslet's *Bantu Folk Tales* was decorated with stylised linocuts by Joyce Wallis to create an 'ethnic' atmosphere. Other books of that era had plenty of monotone drawings done with varying degrees of skill and with what artists conceived of as a 'European' appeal, such as the two drawings by Sheila Hawkins

19

for *The Long Grass Whispers* by Geraldine Elliot (1939), which give all the animals coy human facial expressions. Suddenly, in the 1980s, there was a colour explosion, with true picture books being produced that carefully marry text and polychrome illustrations, great care being given to choice of font and even the shape and size of the book. The publishers of Liguori-Reynolds went for large format, and those of Whitwell, Du Preez and Mhlope used landscape format. The coloured illustrations are more impressionistic in the latest books, using all sorts of techniques. In contrast to the bold approaches of Muzi Donga for Makhuphula's *Xhosa Fireside Tales* and Hargreaves Ntukwana for Mhlope's *The Snake with Seven Heads*, Jack Cope's *Tales of the Trickster Boy* is illustrated very fashionably by Azaria Mbatha with small black- and-white 'naive art' pictures that appear to be linocuts, a style for which he is well known, which resembles that of the celebrated Namibian artist, John Muafangejo. They appear more authentically African than Joyce Wallis's linocuts, but whether or not they appeal to children will have to be left to the children to decide. Another aspect of appearance is the choice of typeface. For *The Snake with Seven Heads*, published by Skotaville, design has overruled practicality: an obscure but very decorative typeface has been used which even skilled readers would find almost illegible, let alone the new readers that Skotaville Publishers, as a black publishing house, hope to encourage.

The implications of translating folktales for children

In evaluating these books I have looked at what their producers claim to be doing and how the books appear to their readers. To conclude the evaluation, one must consider the books in the light of what the whole enterprise of publishing English versions of African (including San) folktales entails. Every step in the transformation of oral performance to final published version moves further away from the true nature of the original towards a product that has a separate existence and significance.

Where children's books have an advantage over academic collections is that they can, and usually do, attempt to reflect the flavour of the original oral delivery. They usually give the narrator a strong voice and personality and even, in some cases (like Savory's Matabele narrator, Chakuti), an historical context. In their dramatic presentations, freed from inhibitions of academic solemnity, writers such as Murgatroyd use questions, exclamations and direct address to the audience to convey something of the atmosphere of the original interplay between narrator and audience. One senses that the writers are actually hoping that their versions will be read aloud – the fact that these are children's books providing a rare opportunity for the oral literary mode to be used. Furthermore, the writers can presume to attempt to convey, in their original form, other elements of the oral delivery such as songs, chants, riddles, repeated phrases, onomatopoeic sounds, and idiosyncrasies of speech that are often excluded or transmuted in more serious translations. Hugh Tracey, in *The Lion on the Path and Other African Stories*, is the reteller who has *par excellence* conveyed these elements of oral performance. Writers can also use devices to suggest a 'long ago and far away' atmosphere, such as storytelling formulae like old Mamethu's 'Now I put this tale back where I found it' (*Tales of the Trickster Boy* 15). Many of the books contribute to the authentic atmosphere by the prolific use of African (and Afrikaans) names and words, riddles, songs and formulae quoted in the original vernacular. Makhuphula includes many songs in Xhosa, with English translation; Savory even gives one song in Xhosa only (*African Fireside Tales* 71).

All this is possible because these books fall within the conventions of books for children. Herein lies also the greatest danger of injustice to the originals and their culture, for the implication might be that African folktales are 'childish'. The old social Darwinist and evolutionist concept of culture used to suggest that preliterate cultures are childish. Albert Lord, one of the greatest scholars of oral tradition, has warned,

> *Outside the circle of folklore enthusiasts the connotations of 'folk' in many countries tend to be derogatory. One thinks of the simple peasant with his 'quaint' ideas, his fairy stories, and children's tales.*[4]

Early travellers in South Africa often went further than simply regarding the inhabitants as childish, by disparagingly equating childishness with crude primitiveness. The Khoekhoen and San

21

were particularly subjected to this sort of vilification. Yet the San produced some of the greatest rock art in the world, and possessed an oral tradition of great complexity and tenderness. W.H.I. Bleek, the ethnographer who recorded their beliefs in the nineteenth century, took a stand against the fashionable social evolutionist theories of his day that provided a rationale for prejudice. He welcomed a paper by J.M. Orpen, which showed how Bushman paintings illustrate Bushman mythology. Orpen's interpretation, he said,

> ... *gives at once to Bushman art a higher character, and teaches us to look upon its products not as the mere daubings of figures for idle pastime, but as an attempt, however imperfect, at a truly artistic conception of the ideas which most deeply moved the Bushman mind and filled it with religious feelings ... A collection of faithful copies of Bushman paintings is, therefore, only second in importance to a collection of their folklore in their own language. Both such collections will serve to illustrate each other, and to contribute jointly towards showing us in its true light the curious mental development of a most remarkable race.*[5]

As long ago as 1914 Sanni Metelerkamp was careful to avoid the implication of childishness: even though old Outa Karel tells his stories to 'my baasjes' and 'noois', she says in her Foreword that her stories are 'sent out to find their own level and take their chance in the workaday world' (ix). Of the modern retellers of the folktales, only Hanneke du Preez openly perpetuates the canard that San culture is childish. She says in her Foreword to *Kgalagadi Tales* that San stories 'are simple, totally free from abstractions – truly primitive art ... Children sense in them a kinship for which there is no rational explanation.'

On the whole the implication that the oral tradition is childish is avoided by the modern writers because much of the material that they select was originally intended for children anyway: as Ruth Finnegan says, in African oral tradition, 'certain stories (perhaps particularly animal stories) are felt to be the preserve of children and to be most suitably told by and to them'.[6] Many of the writers were motivated to publish the stories because they had

22

enjoyed listening to them as children themselves. It is appropriate that these stories should be retold to entertain children.

Apart from the ideological implications of suggesting that San and African folktales are 'primitive', the whole phenomenon of publishing translated children's versions of them in South Africa has also had other ideological functions. Andreé-Jeanne Tötemeyer says,

> The great admiration for African mythology and the culture of blacks in South African juvenile literature, far greater than in any other country of the west, therefore possibly has ideological foundations. The cornerstone of the whole apartheid ideology is the belief in the separate cultural identity of each ethnic group. It is nothing more than the old British 'divide and rule' concept, clad in ethnic attire. By instilling admiration in South African white children for the various black cultures with due emphasis on the differences between them, the apartheid system based on these ethnic differences is perpetuated. Although this may not be the intention of retellers and collectors of Zulu, Swazi, Xhosa, Matabele, Tswana, Tsonga, Venda, Ndebele, Sotho and other ethnic folk tales, their endeavours can contribute to the reinforcement of the concept of ethnicity upon which the apartheid-ideology is based, depending on the manner in which the stories are told.[7]

The 'anthropological approach' of publishers and authors which I have described bears out Tötemeyer's fears about stressing the 'otherness' of the tales.

In contrast to the stories which are traditionally intended for children are stories that obviously had some more profound significance in their original context. The educational functions of African folktales, Scheub says, 'are subtly realised and are not evident to the alien'.[8] Albert Lord concluded in 1960,

> The use of folk stories as entertainment for young children has its ironic aspects; we are beginning to realise the serious symbolism and meaning of folk tales, which, if rightly understood, would be far from proper fare for children.[9]

A further reason why folktales can be unsuitable for children is the frightening nature of their contents. Hugh Tracey comments excitedly in his Foreword to *The Lion on the Path*:

> *Many African stories have such brutal and tragic endings that they can only properly be featured in the case books of psychiatrists, where they should be noted by those students whose idealism for Africa outruns their capacity for realism. (xi)*

It may well be true that, as Savory puts it, 'These African Folk Tales follow very much the same pattern as our European tales, telling of magic and ogres, fairy princes and talking animals, witches and wizards' (*African Fireside Tales Part 1* 171); but English fairy tale books for children cushion their readers against the sort of horrors to be found in African stories. White English-speaking South African children will be familiar with some European folktales, but these have been subjected to varying degrees of bowdlerisation that have removed or disguised the earthiness, cruelty and sexual overtones that were still explicit until the early nineteenth century in versions such as those of Perrault and the Brothers Grimm. Most white children will have been fed on a babyfood of pretty-pretty fairy tales and Walt Disney. However, I do not wish to exaggerate the sensitivities of white children, for their own modern literature – let alone their television viewing – still has its share of nastiness, (in Barrie's *Peter Pan*, C.S. Lewis's Narnia stories, and Roald Dahl, for example) as well as in the deliberate scariness of Maurice Sendak's *Where the Wild Things Are* and the fantasy world of J.R.R. Tolkien, all of which they take in their stride.

Nevertheless, cultural differences pose a challenge to those wishing to build bridges by translating the African tales for English-speaking white children. Whereas traditional European folktales have long been available to children only in their 'art' form, the writers of the English children's versions of African folktales are pioneers, often the first to put the stories in print or make them available to the general public. It would be unfortunate if the writers, in remaining true to their originals, create a garish impression of savagery.

Converting oral tradition to written form is a complex process in which the potential for distortion is great. To begin with, a selection is made, which may not be representative – in the case of these children's books, for example, the selection concentrates on animal stories. To fix in linear printed form a single performance of a narration conveys a misleading notion of the nature of the tradition. To construct what one believes to be the 'essence' of a story, based on several tellings, is to name and shape a new creation according to the expectations and values of the recorder; to shape it in narrative form according to preconceptions of what a story consists of and how it should be told is to hide its meaning, not reveal it. I have already referred to the distortion inherent in the larger enterprise of constructing a cycle of tales. The writing of stories in a style appropriate for children, illustrated and packaged in a book format for children, fixes them in a single context that may not reflect their standing in their own tradition. And once the stories have become reified in print, there may be a temptation for teachers and readers in the future to consider them only as written literature, forgetting their different provenance. I must conclude that although it is not the fault of all those who have published the folktales in the form of children's books, it is a pity that this is almost the only form in which they are known to the reading public, thereby stereotyping the oral tradition as childish. What is needed is serious publishing which will draw upon the resources of modern anthropology to make available to the general reader editions that reflect a greater range and complexity.

The enterprise of publishing translations of folktales is fraught with many pitfalls, some of which we have seen. The motives and attitudes of the writers have varied over the years: early scientific curiosity; cultural superiority; nostalgia – not only for the reteller's childhood but also for a pre-European African paradise; post-colonial guilt with its imperative to make restitution by resuscitating and disseminating for admiration the culture of the colonised; intelligent enjoyment of different cultures together with a wish to build bridges of understanding. In a country where race relations are so delicate, the writers and their publishers have at times been guilty of condescension, misrepresentation or racial stereotyping. Whether they were conscious of it or not, their books have many functions: preserving oral tradition from extinction and bridging the gap between the past and the present, rural and urban, African and Western culture, an oral tradition and a written one.

25

What emerges despite their sometimes fumbling efforts is that these books make a positive contribution to racial harmony and confirm the bond that all South Africans have with their natural environment.

NOTES

1. Emma Bedford, 'Illustrated children's books in South Africa,' in *Doer-land-y/Far far away: South African Illustrated Children's Books*, ed. Marianne Hölscher, Cape Town: South African National Gallery, 1986, 23.
2. Ruth Finnegan, *Oral Literature in Africa*, Oxford: Oxford University Press, 1970, 360.
3. Herbert Vilakazi, 'Educating for the future,' quoted in *Race Relations News*, Dec. 1987, 16.
4. Albert B. Lord, *The Singer of Tales*, Cambridge, Mass.: Harvard University Press, 6.
5. W.H.I. Bleek, 'Remarks on "A glimpse into the mythology of the Maluti Bushmen", by J.M. Orpen', *The Cape Monthly Magazine*, IX:49, July 1874, 13.
6. Finnegan, *Oral Literature in Africa*, 376.
7. Andreé-Jeanne Tötemeyer, 'Impact of African mythology on South African juvenile literature,' *South African Journal of Library and Information Science*, 57:4, December 1989, 397.
8. Harold Scheub, Introduction to *Tales from Southern Africa* by A.C. Jordan, Berkeley: University of California Press, 1973, 2.
9. Lord, *The Singer of Tales*, 6.

CHAPTER TWO

Talking Animals

We animals know that when we die we go to the high pastures where the rain-cows graze and where we will be young once more.
('The apprentice' 67)

Marguerite Poland is South Africa's best-known writer in English for children. From the time that the Percy FitzPatrick Award for South African children's books in English was established by the South African Library Association (now SAILIS) in 1969 and made retrospective to 1964,[1] the first two occasions on which it was awarded were to Marguerite Poland, for *The Mantis and the Moon* in 1979 and *The Wood-ash Stars* in 1984. Six of her books have also received honourable mentions: *Nqalu, the Mouse with No Whiskers* in 1980, *Once at KwaFubesi* in 1981, *Marcus and the Boxing Gloves* in 1986, *Shadow of the Wild Hare* and *The Small Clay Bull* in 1988, and *Marcus and the Go-kart* in 1990. *The Mantis and the Moon* received one of the five Honourable Awards of the Sankei Award for Children's Books in Japan in 1989.

Her joint venture with illustrator Cora Coetzee, *Nqalu, the Mouse with No Whiskers*, won South Africa's leading award for book illustrators, the Katrine Harries Award, in 1979. The award was actually made for the Afrikaans version, *Die Muis Sonder Snorbaard* (1979), which was published before the English version of this, her first book, because in 1979 it was not easy to have a

27

children's book published in South Africa.[2]

Poland has also received recognition as a writer for adults. Her novel, *Train to Doringbult*, was accepted for publication by a British publisher, Bodley Head, and was one of three books shortlisted for the CNA Literary Award in 1988. Most of her books have also been translated into Afrikaans, and some have appeared in African languages. *The Mantis and the Moon* has sold well in Japanese.

Nothing could be more indigenous to South Africa than her life and work. She grew up on an Eastern Cape farm where she acquired a deep knowledge of the Xhosa people, their language and folklore, and the flora and fauna. She obtained her BA Honours in Xhosa at the University of Stellenbosch and an MA in Zulu folklore at the University of Natal.[3] This background, and the careful research she puts into preparing for her writing, are amply evident in her work. Even her experience as a social worker in Port Elizabeth and as a sociologist in Durban has influenced at least one story, the graphic story of urban violence, 'The Windflower'.

Poland is best known for her books for young children. She has also written the adult novel, *Train to Doringbult* (1987), and two novels for young teenagers, the rather unsuccessful *The Bush Shrike* (1982), and the excellent *Shadow of the Wild Hare* (1986), discussed in detail in Chapter Four. Her writing for young children is widely experimental and creative. In one category are her two *Marcus* stories, *Marcus and the Boxing Gloves* (1984) and *Marcus and the Go-kart* (1988). The rest comprise straightforward animal stories, stories about Africans and San (some in the style of folktales) and many stories in which animals, birds and insects are endowed with human qualities. Sometimes her magical animal stories broadly follow traditional lines, such as when they turn out to be *pourquoi* stories (for example, why the mantis holds up his legs in prayer – *The Mantis and the Moon*); at other times they are highly inventive stories of adventure, pathos or knock-about comedy. Her originality and achievement lie in the way she builds the original idea into a rich literary work about rounded characters set in a minutely described milieu, the whole diffused by a unity of vision and narrated in a delicate style. She herself has often said that she hopes that her animal stories, by developing in children a respect for wild creatures, will make them conscious of the need for conservation.

In this chapter I consider her three collections of animal stories: *The Mantis and the Moon* (1979), *Once at KwaFubesi* (1981), and *Sambane's Dream and Other Stories* (1989).[4] The Penguin volume, *Sambane's Dream and Other Stories*, is a revised edition of the two earlier volumes, omitting three stories and adding two new ones. Poland admits in her Preface that the stories needed pruning; but their re-issue prompted further argument as to whether, in spite of being given the approval of the Percy Fitz-Patrick Award, these stories are actually popular with children. One reviewer of *Sambane's Dream*, for example, said:

> *Some of the stories are simple and effective, such as 'The smallest chief', which is one of the new ones, but others are a little drawn-out and wordy, and sometimes even quite clumsy, and as the book was written for children, this might not be the best way of holding their attention.*[5]

Jay Heale, South Africa's best known commentator on the children's book scene, looking back over the decade since they were first published, concluded,

> *Many children have enjoyed them; many have found them over-long and over-wordy. Yet read aloud, in selected extracts, they will thrill young listeners with their accurate details of South African wildlife, the lively characters of the creatures, and the polished poetical writing.*[6]

Heale calls *Sambane's Dream* a 'precious volume' and a 'memorable collection'. Whatever its fate at the hands of children, it is writing of remarkable quality.

In all the stories of these three books animals are central. Most of the stories create a fantasy world in which animals can talk and possess, to varying degrees, other human characteristics. In writing this kind of story, Poland is working within two traditions: the oral tradition of African and San folktales, and the 'art' versions of the old 'talking beast' tales of Europe, with their descendants, modern children's stories which depict anthropomophised animals. We have already seen that she is one of a number of South African children's writers who, in the 1980s and 1990s, write stories 'in the style of' indigenous folktales. As soon as a writer does this, she invites comparison not only with her original models, but also with the literary genre of folktales which has, over many centuries, developed norms and therefore expectancies among its readers. Her own account of the influences on her writing points to these two sources:

> *Like most English-speaking children I was raised on Beatrix Potter, A.A. Milne and Alison Uttley – but the hares, hedgehogs and mice in their tales were different in character from the ones I knew. On the other hand, there was the community of characters which I had come to know through studying the African folk tale – Mbulu, the monitor lizard, Thenetya, the red hare, and the trickster Chakide, the slender mongoose … I have always been fascinated by the beliefs of the San (Bushmen). And from some of these have come inspiration for my stories.[7]*

Elsewhere, she says that her favourite book as a child was Alison Uttley's *Little Grey Rabbit*.[8]

Before going on to look at Poland's own contribution, let us consider the two traditions in which she was working.

The European tradition

The traditional talking beast fables of Europe were of various kinds. The earliest were folklore and fairy tales, full of magic; later they became fables, composed for instruction or amusement – such as *pourquoi* stories or those which pointed a moral – or they entertained with the antics of well-loved characters such as Reynard the Fox which nevertheless also constituted a shrewd commentary on human foibles. In medieval times the use of animals as 'emblems' developed, and the literature was systematised into 'bestiaries' and 'fables'. Among the rhetorical principles governing the writing of fables was *prosopopeia*, whereby human language is given to beings that have no power of speech. Chaucer had this in mind when he wrote *The Nun's Priest's Tale*:

> *For thilke tyme, as I have understonde,*
> *Bestes and briddes coude speke and synge.[9]*

His tale, like all fables, carried a lesson:

> *But ye that holden this tale a folye*
> *As of a fox, or of a cok and hen,*
> *Taketh the moralitee, good men.*[10]

Bestiaries and fables endowed animals with a single characteristic, supposedly coinciding with that animal's nature, which caricatured some human vice, folly or virtue. Chaucer's subtlety in *The Nun's Priest's Tale* lies in the ironic interplay of human traits and the obviously animal traits of Chauntecleer and Pertelote. Similarly, the moral of *Animal Farm* by George Orwell does not lie simply in the ending, but in the interaction, in this case the disgusting effect of seeing animals behave as depraved human beings.

After the fables and bestiaries, a third stage that traditional folktales went through in Europe was the romantic period epitomised by Hans Christian Andersen which opened the way for the new animal fantasies of the twentieth century. Modern English children's stories in this tradition have continued to make witty play of the congruities and incongruities of animal and human traits. To be effective, the animal must still be seen to possess some dominant human characteristic. Thus in *The Wind in the Willows* by Kenneth Grahame we take pleasure in recognising a badger who is avuncular and lives in an underground house, and it seems natural to us that the stoats and weasels are the crooks; nevertheless we are also delighted by the surprise of seeing Toad as a madcap daredevil. Many children's stories continue to capitalise on this interplay of identification and contrast. When an animal has one dominant characteristic, much of the pleasure for the young reader comes from anticipating the character's behaviour as the plot unfolds, and recognising that behaviour when it occurs. The toy-animal characters of A.A. Milne's *Winnie-the-Pooh* and Michael Bond's *Paddington* stories are good examples.

However, there are also many stories in which the animals are much more complex, and therefore humanlike. Traditional nursery stories and modern animal stories for children contain varying degrees of anthropomorphism. At the lowest end of the scale are animals which are animals in every recognisable way except that they have the power of speech, and even that is limited to utterances of a suitably limited intelligence or range of perception: Mowgli's companions in Kipling's *Jungle Book* stories are an example. From that point we find a progression through the possession of human traits. In the twentieth century this has included the gross sentimentality of imputing human emotions to animals in *Bambi* by Felix Stalten; and the creation of Walt Disney's Mickey Mouse and Donald Duck, who dress, live, behave and talk in an almost entirely human manner. Some recent children's stories have introduced typically twentieth century slants to the anthropomorphism in order to point to a new kind of moral: in *Mrs Frisby and the Rats of NIMH* by R.C. O'Brien, the rats are given their superintelligence and physical skills while kept captive as the subjects of scientific experiments in the NIMH laboratories (though this does not account for the traditional fantasy of the power of speech possessed by the rats and Mrs Frisby, the mouse), in Russell Hoban's *The Mouse and His Child* the central character is a *clockwork* mouse endowed with a soul and the power of speech, who mixes with talking animals. These stories point to the consequences of human beings' responsibility as creators and interferers in creation.

Because there is such a long, pervasive tradition of talkinganimal stories and because human beings are so ready to suspend their disbelief, readers accept these modern stories; but not all modern stories handle anthropomorphism with the same degree of success. Success depends upon whether the writers are able to create a consistent fantasy world – as Aristotle put it, 'A likely impossibility is always preferable to an unconvincing possibility'.[11] Generally, the weakness lies in the treatment of human beings and human artefacts. That the anthropomorphised animals live in a man-made environment is not in itself a problem: the laboratories of NIMH, and the farmyard with its barns that forms the setting of *Charlotte's Web* by E.B. White, are good examples. However, if the animals encounter human beings it can be utterly incongruous. Anderson and Groff, in discussing criteria for good children's books, remark approvingly of *Charlotte's Web* that 'it is also significant that the animals talk only to each other and never to human beings'.[12] I consider *Watership Down* ruined when, after Richard Adams has built up a consistent, plausible society of talking rabbits, he suddenly introduces human beings who talk among themselves and pick rabbits up, reminding the reader that rabbits are really only small pests. Margaret Blount, in her exhaustive book, *Animal Land: the Creatures of Children's Fiction*, dislikes most those stories in which humans and animals are indistinguishable, inhabiting the same world; she prefers stories in which the animals, even if they can speak, 'do what animals always do'.[13]

There is a further type of talking animal story in which convention allows animals and humans to converse. These stories do not portray animal society such as in *Charlotte's Web* and *Watership Down*. Human beings instead play a large, often central part, and their relationship with animals is governed by magic. Thus, Puss in Boots talks to human beings, much to their surprise. Many African folktales are of this kind.

The tradition of African folktales

The European tradition of talking-animal stories has gone through three stages, traditional folktales and nursery stories, 'art' versions of these, and modern children's stories. African animal stories to which the English-speaking reader has access are still roughly at the oral stage. The English versions of southern African folktales that have been published for children are fairly unsophisticated retellings which keep close to the orally transmitted originals. As far as modern southern African literature featuring talking animals is concerned, there is little worth remembering.

Many African talking-animal stories are like the traditional European ones in having aetiological or trickster plots, but they do not often take the form of explicitly didactic moral fables, and Marguerite Poland usually follows the African tradition in this regard, although she does sometimes like to end a story with a neatly phrased aphorism. Both the later stories added to *Sambane's Dream and Other Stories* end in this way. 'The smallest chief', for example, concludes,

> ... *it is not by strength or cunning or by might that rulers shall be made, but by the wisdom which is found when the small, still voice inside the heart is heard. (206)*

There are also African folktales in which human beings, animals and even objects such as bowls converse with each other through magic, and Poland has followed this style successfully in one story, 'Child of the Doves' (*The Wood-ash Stars* 51). However, I shall restrict my comments to her stories in which the characters are all animals.

33

Poland's stories in the light of European and African traditions

It is enlightening to consider Poland's stories against the background of European and African traditions. San folktales provide further perspectives which will be considered later. As might be expected, Poland's settings are much fuller than those in traditional folktales. They are also extremely accurately described.

One cannot help feeling that some of Poland's contemporaries by comparison are rather cavalier in their treatment of the African countryside. For example, though purporting to be re-telling tales of ancient times. Pitcher in *The Calabash Child* writes of weeping willows, and Murgatroyd in *Tales From the Kraals* writes of blackjacks – both are items of exotic vegetation that jar in the context.

Poland has three different settings for her stories, her favourite being the Eastern Cape where she grew up:

> *It was a quiet valley between a scoop of hills and dunes. A valley where the tracks of duiker traced back and forth across the ash-grey sand and bushbuck kept to the thickets. Tortoises plied from ghaukum patch to ghaukum patch and drongoes and hoopoes and dusky bushbirds lived there. Only in spring the bright electric flash and sweet, piercing note of bee-eaters livened up the bush when they came to nest in the limestone banks. It was a place where the cicadas shrilled among the blombos when the summer bergwind blew; where mist drifted in winter, salty with sea-spray, and the thickets which grew down to the beach were bent and twisted from turning their backs to the gale. And it was called KwaFubesi by those who lived there – the home of the giant eagle-owl. (85)*

Her care over detail, her use of colourful popular names for plants and creatures and her well-chosen adjectives give an extraordinary sense of particularity to her settings. This is the Drakensberg:

> *The steep hills rose up towards a rim of sandstone cliffs. The bottlebrushes across the stream were bright with red*

flowers and among the mtshitshi bushes they could see a
herd of sand-coloured eland browsing. (47)

Her third setting is the desert:

> *He reached the undulating razorbacks of the dunes where*
> *he saw the frail-feathered tracks of mice and beetles in the*
> *sand. (76)*
>   *The gazelle-star longs for the season when the rain re-*
> *awakens the desert and the tsha and tsama melons swell on*
> *their slim, green vines; when the acacias burst their bark*
> *and press out the amber beads of gum and the sha roots*
> *ripening beneath the earth are sweet and firm. (80)*

Poland is circumspect in the introduction of human elements into
her landscapes. She keeps the focus firmly on the animals. Once
one has accepted the fantasy that these animals can talk, we find
that they live in an authentic and entirely recognisable world,
where the correct scale and proportions are preserved. Into this
world it is to be expected that people should intrude, but they are
simply one of the many forces that affect the animals' lives: they
build dams that flood valleys, they clear the bush and grow crops
that the bushpigs covet, they built and then abandoned the farmyard where a family of rats dwell. The farmer who fires at the
jackal Mpungutye is a phenomenon as inexplicable to the animal
as the mists of the sea. When the man and his dogs hunt the bushpigs in 'Once at KwaFubesi', the man is seen externally and
briefly, with none of the incongruity caused by the introduction of
human beings in *Watership Down*.
    I have already remarked on the subtle manner in which animal
stories can make social comment through playing on the similari-
ties and dissimilarities between animals and human beings, as in
The Nun's Priest's Tale. Poland uses the interplay between the microcosm of the animals' world and the macrocosm of the real-life
setting to similar effect in a remarkable story, 'The Windflower'.
The world to which the country spider, Lwembu, is persuaded to
elope is a rubble-heap in a city, and the life of the rubble-heap
reflects the life of the city. The heap is ugly and stinks, 'sour with
the smell of wet ash' (154). In this repulsive, alien environment
the blackjack weed takes its rightful place:

Then she crept out and climbed the blackjack weed that grew near the web, following the brightness of a street-lamp … looking for the moon. (153)

Life in the heap resembles the life that a black rural immigrant would encounter in the city, crowded and noisy with 'the faint scufflings of feet outside, cries and voices' (154). The inhabitants are hostile and worldly-wise, and everyone goes in fear of the gangsters:

She had heard the tramp of feet and crouched down, not daring to move. Six large spiders had slouched by. Their legs were banded black and yellow and bristled with stiff spines. They had fierce jaws and they glanced about with a multitude of hooded eyes, snapping up moths and flies with frightening ease and talking to each other in the cool banter of those who are afraid of no one. (151)

The achievement of this indictment of city life is unparalleled in children's animal stories. The plot, in outline, might be hackneyed, and so may the message (of the purity of the countryside), but her ability to embody so many facets of macrocosmic city life in such authentic yet appropriate components of the microcosmic rubble-heap is an exceptional creative feat.

The characters of Poland's stories, like her settings, are usually much fuller than those in traditional tales. A good example is Sidenge the hare, in the story 'Sidenge's potion'. This is an original story based on the traditional African folk theme of the hare as trickster, but Sidenge is an endearing young creature whose life is much more complex than that of Kalulu, Vundhla, Mmutla, Brer Rabbit, or any other of hare's traditional personifications. Typically of Poland, the story is filled with incidental details that enrich the basic plot: for example, although Sidenge is a would-be diviner, we learn in passing of his frailty:

Slowly he gathered the ingredients together, wrinkling his nose at the pungent smell of puffadder fat, leguaan scales and river-slime. (145)

She is skilful at using understatement to suggest the emotional

36

state of the animal characters. 'Gada's pool', for example, is a moving story about a pair of sandgrouse and how they protect their chicks from a bushcat, in which their brief conversations and their actions are sufficient to convey their mutual love. In the convincing world created by the stories, the fate of even the smallest creatures grips the reader, such as when the little ant-eating chat, Nzwili, faces his killers to make amends for having betrayed his friend Sambane:

> And Nzwili, unafraid, stood upright as he always has, upright and he sang his song of praise, 'piek, piek, piek', for who can fear his fellows when his heart is given to a star? (15)

Part of the unique identity of the characters comes from their names. In an appendix to *Once at KwaFubesi* Poland tells us that they 'are derived from the Xhosa, Zulu, Tswana, San (Bushman) and Shona languages' (150). Some are the African names for species, such as 'Ntini' for 'otter'; others are common nouns such as 'Thamba' – 'gentle one', and even onomatopoeic words such as 'Mokhwara' – 'shortened form of the sound made by a sandgrouse'. The use of African names and words makes the family of Mbiba the rat in 'If the boerboon flowers fall' almost undiscernibly a Xhosa family. There are hints that the language in which these talking rats converse is actually Xhosa. We hear the old man, Xhego, muttering: 'Bean bread and bean soup ... Mbiba's wife will say "What a feast, Xhego!" ... and I will say "Nkosikazi, may my ancestors bless you" '(59). So true to the Xhosa does Poland keep that in the original versions of the stories, the prolific use of Xhosa and Zulu words could have been an obstacle to an English-speaking reader, but she has reduced their use considerably in the revised versions.

She also uses Afrikaans words, usually the popular South African names of flora, fauna and topographical features such as 'wit-els', 'rhebok' and 'donga'. These terms occur in such an incidental way that they add to the marvellously indigenous flavour of the stories without being conspicuous. Unfortunately, she occasionally has to use more technical or scientific names for the purposes of the story, and these strike one as incongruous. Examples are the 'pompilid wasp' (141), an important feature in

'Sidenge's potion', and the climax to the story 'The season of the stubby caterpillar', where it is essential for the moth to be identified, but it sounds strange that one of the creatures of the forest (none of whom knows that caterpillars turn into moths) should exclaim, 'A Silver Spotted Ghost Moth!' when he sees her.

(This story, which appeared in *The Mantis and the Moon*, is not included in *Sambane's Dream and Other Stories*.)

At the opposite end of the spectrum to the fully rounded characters are two animal stories in which the central animals are given names, but not the power of speech. In 'The great tusker' the elephant is, however, endowed with near-human thought:

> *Nzou broke into an uneasy run – then stopped, annoyed. Why should he hurry – he, who had seen almost sixty seasons of summer storms and in the shadow of whose side young elephants had sheltered from the wind? (184)*

I prefer 'Mpungutye – the story of a jackal', in which the imputing of thought and emotion to the jackal is restrained. The actions of the jackal are usually seen from the outside, and when reasons for the animal's behaviour are given, the effect is credible: 'Mpungutye stops, lowering his head to the ground. There is a scent belonging to man …' (70); and 'He raises his head, his ears laid back, and cries in anguish. "Tsa, tsa, tsa" ' (74). The action of the story is a completely plausible wild life story, which is nevertheless full of pathos for the reader, precisely because we feel the vulnerability of mere animals in their harsh environment.

The tradition of San folktales

'Mpungutye – the story of a jackal' is one of the small number of Poland's stories told in the San, rather than African, style. This story is of a kind not found in San folklore – it is straightforward and non-magical, typical of twentieth-century Western culture with its concern for animal welfare and conservation. But it has elements of San-style of storytelling, such as the use of the present tense, which resembles the diction of San stories when directly translated into English; and it makes reference to San mythology, for example: '"Tsa! Tsa! Tsa!" they reply, calling to him as he hunts the star-herds in their journey through the sky' (79).

38

In writing stories in the style of the San, Poland was entering a field less well known than African folktales. Only a few translations of San folktales have been published. Some examples are *With Uplifted Tongue* and *The Rebirth of the Ostrich* by A. Markowitz and *Bushman Stories* by E.W. Thomas, which were not particularly intended for children, and the children's books, *The Bushmen and their Stories* by Elizabeth Helfman, published in the USA, and *Kgalagadi Tales* by Hanneke du Preez. There are probably more Afrikaans than English translations.

Another approach to conveying San tales to white children was taken by Mary Phillips in two books which she published in the 1960s, but it proved a dead end which has not been emulated since. In *The Bushman Speaks* (1961) and *The Cave of Uncle Kwa: a Bushman Fantasy* (1965), she creates bands of fictional San, with a central child character, set in the sixteenth and seventeenth centuries, and in the course of describing their adventures she has the characters relate their myths. (Little Ko, the central child character, even tells them to his pet lion cub as they walk through the veld). Her books have become dated in style and approach and make tedious reading, not helped by the poor illustrations. Her account of how rock art was produced and what it signified has been rendered obsolete by research that began in the 1960s, notably that of David Lewis-Williams.[14] (Poland's account of rock art in 'The apprentice' is very similar to Mary Phillips's, which is less forgivable, since her story was written, and later revised, much more recently.)

English versions of San myths are dominated by those of Dorothea Bleek, particularly *The Mantis and His Friends* (1923), which are near-literal translations of tales transcribed by her father, Dr W.H.I. Bleek, in the 1860s. Most other retellings of San tales have maintained the quaint phraseology and syntax of the Bleek translations, and Poland also uses this diction to some extent in an invented legend ('The rainbulls'):

Storms are brought by the rain-bulls. The rain-cows come with the misty showers of summer. They are a great herd of eland that live in the sky-pastures ... That is where their herder, the wind, keeps them until winter has gone ... Only a little water will have fallen, and the desert, thinking it is spring, will put forth its green leaves and shoots. (80)

The short sentences, appositive phrases, and present participles are typical of this style. However, Poland is restrained in her use of the archaic style, compared with the excesses of some other retellers of African and San folktales, like E.W. Thomas, who uses expressions such as 'my heart, strangely moved', 'what manner of tree', and 'made answer',[15] and Markowitz, with his 'thee's', 'thou's' and 'shalt's'.

San tales usually feature talking animals. But anyone proposing to imitate these stories is faced with a paradox regarding the nature of their anthropomorphism, for the San are ambiguous as to whether the characters are to be regarded as talking animals or human beings and spirits with animal names. This affects the characters' speech, their use of human accoutrements, and whether we can expect to find the usual interplay of stereotyped animal traits and human nature. The San regarded the animal characters in their stories as human beings, 'people of the early race':

> *The Blue Crane was also a person of the early race. She was the Mantis's eldest sister. The girls were girls of the early race ... The Frog was a person; her husband was a person; the Blue Crane was a person. They were people of the early race.*[16]

Hence animals of different species could be related and they could, in addition to possessing magical powers, do things that humans do: 'The young man Tick was silent. He lifted the pot away and put it nicely on the fire';[17] 'The Mantis said ,"This person sounds as if he were tipsy".'[18]

There is little connection between an animal's species and its behaviour in the stories, except perhaps for size – Ichneumon and Springbuck being children.

The paradox in the San view of these characters as humans becomes apparent when one considers some remarkable information given by Bleek:

> *A curious feature of Bushman folklore is the peculiar speech attributed to certain animals and to the Moon. It is an attempt at imitating the shape or position of the mouth of the animal in question. As a rule clicks are changed into other special clicks, or into other consonants.*[19]

So, although there is almost nothing in the stories to indicate that
the characters are animals or the moon, they do not speak like
human beings. In introducing the story of the Moon and the Hare,
Bleek remarks, 'The most difficult click of all is the one used by
the Moon, the Hare and the Anteater.'[20] The narrator of this story
says,

> *He is the Moon. Therefore he tells the Moon's story, he
> does not tell a person's story, for thus he speaks, he tells
> the Moon's stories ... The Hare speaks the Hare's lan-
> guage, he speaks like this.*[21]

There is an amusing scene in the story of 'The mantis and the
elephants' which illustrates the differences between the speech of
different animals. The Elephant has carried off the little Springbuck, leaving the Elephant's calf behind in its place to be fed by
Mantis:

> *The Mantis was digging out wild bees' honey and throwing
> it to the little Springbuck. He said: 'Are you eating, as I
> am eating?' The little Springbuck was silent and did not
> answer the Mantis. The Mantis said: 'What is the matter
> that the child does not speak to me, when I ask whether it
> is eating as I too am eating?' Then the Elephant calf said:
> 'Kurru!' And the Mantis said: 'Listen! What is the matter?
> My child does not usually speak so that I cannot under-
> stand it. Let me take out more honey and throw it out
> again, so that I may hear whether it is my child speaking;
> for I do not understand what this child answers; I do not
> hear plainly.'*[22]

The dialogue in all talking animal stories is crucial, and even in
European tradition it was usually thought that the animals should
have a characteristic way of speaking. Oliver Goldsmith made this
point when he got the better of Dr Johnson in an exchange recorded by Boswell:

> *Sir Joshua Reynolds was in company with them one day,
> when Goldsmith said, that he thought he could write a
> good fable, mentioned the simplicity which that kind of*

41

*composition requires, and observed that in most fables the
animals introduced seldom talk in character. 'For instance
(said he,) the fable of the little fishes, who saw birds fly
over their heads, and envying them, petitioned Jupiter to
be changed into birds. The skill (continued he,) consists in
making them talk like little fishes.' While he indulged himself in this fanciful reverie, he observed Johnson shaking
his sides, and laughing. Upon which he smartly proceeded,
'Why, Dr Johnson, this is not so easy as you seem to think:
for if you were to make little fishes talk, they would talk
like WHALES.'*[23]

If Marguerite Poland had closely imitated San stories, therefore,
we might have expected her animal characters to have a distinct
way of speaking, but in other respects to be indistinguishable from
humans. However, in some ways her stories are the reverse of
authentic San ones. For one thing, her animal characters are read-
ily identifiable as true animals. She even goes so far as to
distinguish between the two different kinds of otter found in the
Drakensberg. Furthermore, the dialogue of her animal characters is
not some special 'animal' dialect, but conventional human speech.
She even avoids the literary convention of archaic speech.

The only exceptions, which no doubt would have pleased
Goldsmith, are a few creatures of the bush who play an incidental
role in the stories, serving more as authentic background than as
characters: ' "Ah, ah, ah, ah, ah, ah, ah, there is no time, no time,
no time," chanted the wood-dove from a thicket' (93); 'Fubesi the
giant eagle owl inspected the tracks that led downward through the
loose sand. "Hu, huuu, hu huuu," he cried' (105); and 'A gecko,
disturbed from his sleep on the wall, bobbed up and down in
alarm. "Gick, gick, gick! The Zindlavini!" he cried' (155).

Poland's animals are also unlike the animals in traditional
European and African fables, which are usually stereotyped as
having only one major trait, such as cunning or greed. Each animal in her stories is seen as an individual, perhaps because she
knows too much about natural history to be satisfied with fanciful
typecasting. As it is not a part of her method or purpose to play on
human/ animal parallels for didactic purposes, we find that the
personality with which she endows each individual is largely arbitrary. Whereas Reynard the Fox is always associated with cunning,

the patient old fellow who paints the rock painting in 'The apprentice' might just as well (and even more appropriately) have been a dassie as a hare. This arbitrary association of character traits and animal species makes her stories much closer to San tales.

Although Poland's animals are much more obviously *animals* than those in San folktales, she endows them with a distinctly San flavour, just as her family of rats in 'If the boerboon flowers fall' is identifiably Xhosa. Consequently, her San-style stories follow her models by strongly suggesting that the animal characters are 'people of the early race'. In 'Tusi and the dry wind' the animals hold San beliefs:

> *The eland move out of the dune country, birds flock from the empty water-courses and the herds of springbok travel east, leaving behind the old or the very young and weak. That is the law of the desert – nor do the old ones fear it, for close behind the last migration of the herds a small dry wind comes, gently spiralling the sand. 'There tracks the dry wind,' they say. 'It has come to take us to the sky-plains where the Gauun flowers grow.' (168)*

The 'comfort song of springbok mothers' also contains San words:

> *A-ahn! A-ahn!*
> *Wai! Springbok child, sleep for me.*
> *Wai! Springbok child, sleep for me. (169)*

The aardvark, Sambane, in 'Sambane's dream', is clearly a San. She communes with the star Xkoagu, who brings forth the termites which Sambane eats. Poland prefaces this story and 'The apprentice' with epigraphs taken from the versions of Bleek's transcriptions included in the *Penguin Book of South African Verse*, implying that the animals hold authentic San beliefs:

> *Xkoagu, give me your heart,*
> *that you sit with in plenty.*
> *Take my heart, my heart*
> *small and famished without hope*
> *so that like you I too may be full*
> *for I hunger. (1)*

43

'Sambane would dream a dream of ants', and after eating she gives a prayer of thanksgiving: 'Guriko !gum, guriko !gum' (1).

In 'The apprentice', which I consider her best San-style story, the hares who paint on the walls of the Drakensberg caves are almost indistinguishable from San, in spite of having the physical appearance and feeding habits of hares. They hold the same religious beliefs, and recall that their ancestors were taught to paint by the now-vanished San, whose traditions they maintain. Later the old hare says, 'Our ancestor himself was once that San child' (67), thus making the identification complete. The result is an intriguing fantasy world, neither human nor animal.

The human accoutrements which Poland's animals use are generally the same as those in the San folktales — ropes, cudgels, bags, a few utensils. Here she is on potentially dangerous ground if she wishes to maintain the Aristotelian principle of plausibility. In a story like 'The apprentice' one does not notice the use of paints, brushes and paint boxes made of horn tips, for the hares are, as Dorothea Bleek says of the Mantis, 'just a sort of dream Bushman';[24] but the otter's playing of a reed flute is slightly incongruous. Poland's animals are not so anthropomorphised as Kenneth Grahame's or Beatrix Potter's, so if the fantasy is to be complete, these details have to be underplayed. Fortunately, they normally are. In the whole of 'The windflower', in spite of its urban setting, the creatures do not use a single artefact.

The original quality of Poland's stories

The plots of Poland's stories are, as one might expect, far more tightly knit than San and African folktales. The tone of each story is also more clearly defined, to suit the modern Western reader, so that we can distinguish drama, adventure, comedy and pathos. Because they are set so inextricably in the southern African context, even where she uses stock situations or themes she is making an original contribution to southern African literature. In concluding this look at the stories, here are two quotations to convey their flavour: one of comedy, the other of pathos.

In her story of broad comedy, 'Sidenge's potion', she gives her own touch to the old plot of the misapplied love potion, with ludicrous consequences when the old hare finds himself being serenaded: ' "Ah, my chosen one," called the polecat melodiously'

(138). By contrast, many of her stories have an air of melancholy. Common themes are old age, loss, the approach of death, rebirth, regeneration and the succession of the younger generation. These are encapsulated in the ending of the story 'Once at KwaFubesi' in which the family, or "sounder', of bushpigs is driven from its old territory:

> *The stars were fading and the low bush was black with night-shadow. The sounder moved off, keeping the steady shuffle-pace of Nungu and Mnci. On and on they went, following the trail to the wide river where shy bushbuck and dusky bushbirds lived. Only once did Nduna stop. He stood apart, listening for the last time to the deep, familiar call of his home: the cry of Fubesi, the giant eagle owl, 'hu huuu, hu huuu,' mourning from the flatlands where the sweet-thorn grew.*
>
> *Nduna stood in the gathering silence and then he turned to the waiting sounder and said, 'Bomvu, lead us on. This will be your territory to defend. Lead us on, my son.'*
>
> *Bomvu looked back at his father for a long moment. Then, crest raised on his strong young shoulders, he led them westwards to where the slow, wide river reached out to the sea. (110)*

Marguerite Poland's 'Stories for the children of Africa' are unique to their time and place. They are not the moral fables that their European talking-beast ancestors were; nor do they reflect the concerns, almost uninterpretable to modern anthropologists, of their San and African cousins. If we are to search for the didactic message of her stories, this is what we find: that in the animal world we can see, on a short time-scale, processes of death and change that have been sanitised out of the Western child's life. She teaches that it is legitimate to grieve over change, but the vitality and regeneration of the animal world show us also how to hope.

NOTES

1. Anna Louw, 'The Percy FitzPatrick Award for children's books,' *CRUX*, 11:2, April 1977.

2. *Fairlady*, 'African fantasy,' January 1984, 11.

3. Joan Gallagher, 'The creator of animal fairy-tales – Marguerite Poland,' *Artes Natales*, April 1983, 8, 10.

4. All quotations and page references for the stories are taken from *Sambane's Dream and Other Stories*, Harmondsworth: Penguin, 1989.

5. *Pretoria News*, 'Two tales added to animal stories,' review of *Sambane's Dream and Other Stories* by 'S.M.', 29 October 1990.

6. Jay Heale, 'South African books,' *Bookchat*, 94, May 1990, 27.

7. Marguerite Poland, 'Do local children still believe in pink elephants?' *Sunday Times Magazine*, 14 March 1982, 5.

8. Gorry Bowes-Taylor, 'The mouse grows whiskers,' *The Argus*, 22 September 1983, 15.

9. Geoffrey Chaucer, *The Nonne Preestes Tale*, in *The Complete Works of Geoffrey Chaucer*, ed. W.W. Skeat, Oxford: Oxford University Press, 1912, ll 60-61.

10. Chaucer, *The Nonne Preestes Tale*, ll 658-660.

11. Aristotle, *On the Art of Poetry*, trans. Ingram Bywater, Oxford: The Clarendon Press, 1920, 84.

12. W. Anderson and P. Groff, *A New Look at Children's Literature*, Belmont: Wadsworth, 1972, 90.

13. Margaret Blount, *Animal Land: The Creatures of Children's Fiction*, London: Hutchinson, 1974, 259.

14. See, for example, J.D. Lewis-Williams, *Discovering Southern African Rock Art*, Cape Town: David Philip, 1990.

15. E.W. Thomas, *Bushman Stories*, Cape Town: Oxford University Press, 1950, 50, 29, 28.

16. D.F. Bleek, ed., *The Mantis and his Friends: Bushman Folklore*, collected by the late Dr W.H.I. Bleek and the late Dr Lucy C. Lloyd, Cape Town: Maskew Miller, 1923, 23, 26.

17. Bleek, *The Mantis and his Friends*, 30.

18. Bleek, *The Mantis and his Friends*, 53.

19. D.F. Bleek, 'Special speech of animals and moon used by the /Xam bushmen,' *Bantu Studies*, X, 1936, 163.

20. Bleek, 'Special speech of animals', 186.

21. Bleek, 'Special speech of animals', 186.

22. Bleek, *The Mantis and his Friends*, 41.

23. J. Boswell, *The Life of Samuel Johnson*, 3 vols., London, Swan Sonnenschein, Lowrey & Co., 1888, 466.

24. Bleek, *The Mantis and his Friends*, ii.

CHAPTER THREE

The Bushveld Syndrome

The publication and contents of children's books dealing with life in South Africa reflect the social history of English speakers in the country. In the nineteenth century, adventure books for boys set in South Africa were published in Britain, aimed at a British readership, and heavily weighted with both scientific information on the country's botany, geography, history and so on, and with moralising on topics such as the responsibilities of British colonisers towards the native races. There was no thought of writing books for white South African children, since colonials were expected to receive an education that was British in every respect. State and private schools that were established in South Africa towards the end of the imperial era were modelled on British public schools, which by that stage had developed into efficient training institutions for providing the manpower to administer the British Empire.

The nature and values of the public schools had changed during the nineteenth century. Early reformers such as the famous Dr Arnold of Rugby had emphasised Christian character-building – an ideal portrayed by Dean Farrar in his boys' story, *Eric, or Little by Little* (1858). But as the century progressed the emphasis changed to 'muscular Christianity', or indeed, simply muscularity. South African schools were staffed by expatriate British schoolmasters and schoolmistresses, and took on all the trappings of their British models: 'houses', prefects, uniforms, compulsory games, corporal punishment and military cadets for the boys, a classical curriculum, and the old school network.

Following the Second Anglo-Boer War, the effort to maintain the Englishness of South African schools reached new heights under the inspiration of Lord Milner. Actually, in some respects the philistine late public school model suited South Africa. As Mangan comments about the schools of the Empire,

> *Educational aims valued so highly at other times and in other contexts, such as the development of an inquiring mind, independence of thought and the questioning of established orthodoxies, were unacceptable in an environment of primitive backwardness.*[1]

And Honey has argued that the elitism of the system was 'functionally appropriate to the existing social and political system of South Africa'.[2] However, the ideal continued to be the English model but, much to the discomfort of educators, the South Africanism of the children kept on showing through. G.M.H. Bobbins, a prominent South African English teacher of the 1930s and 1940s, wrote a book deploring their poor English, which he entitled *The Twilight of English*,[3] and his despair was echoed by Montague J. Rendall, former Headmaster of Winchester. Rendall championed public school ideals through his work on the Rhodes Trust and as Chairman of the Public Schools Empire Tours Committee from 1926-1939, an organisation that sent parties of British public schoolboys around the Empire to propagate their values. Here is his comment on Rhodesian and South African schoolboys:

> *If I were to design a medal for one of these Schoolboys the superscription might be 'Child of the Sun'; the obverse a figure of 'independence with a Shield', or perhaps 'Venator Intrepidus', like Pisanello's model of Alphonso the Magnanimous, where a naked boy is riding astride of a fearsome boar; but a Lion to replace the Boar, and the reverse should be just a bright Star to symbolise the Sun, 'radiatum insigne diei'. The rest of the field would consist of several Rugby footballs and a scanty heap of books. For*

*indeed, truth to tell, this wholesome brown boy, with khaki
shirt, khaki shorts and a pair of rough shoes, who looks
straight at you from rather wild eyes half-hidden in a mat
of hair, is just a Child of the Sun ... They are by nature
Children of the Sun, Sun-worshippers, and Culture has little meaning for them. Why should parents and
schoolmasters disturb this happy dream? Why worry the
boys with Culture? Well, this is the plea of all children
since Cain and Abel first worshipped the Sun in the morning of the world, a plea urged with childish impertinence
and irresistible grace; but these Schools are not meant for
Mowgli.[4]*

With this kind of reluctance to see white South African children as
belonging in their own setting, it is small wonder that only a handful of English language South African children's books appeared
in the first half of the twentieth century. Reference works on South
African English literature obviously have had to scratch to find
early children's fiction that they could list: Malvern van Wyk
Smith in *Grounds of Contest* does not mention any (under popular
writers the only books that he refers to that could be said to be
suitable for children are the non-fiction works of Victor Pohl);[5] the
Companion to South African English Literature lists three or four
up to 1965 that are 'worth noting';[6] and Jay Heale 'recalls' only
Pohl's *Farewell the Little People* and 'several books by Mary Phillips'.[7] South Africa does not have its children's classic of pioneer
fiction to match *Anne of Green Gables* in Canada, *Little House on
the Prairie* in the USA, and *Seven Little Australians* in Australia.
The nearest are the two adult classics – the children's episodes in
Olive Schreiner's *The Story of an African Farm* (1883), and
Platkops Children (1935) by Pauline Smith.

Appropriately, considering Rendall's characterisation of the
South African boy as 'venator intrepidus' – 'intrepid hunter/sports-
man' – one book stands out as the most famous South African
children's book: Percy FitzPatrick's *Jock of the Bushveld* (1907).
At face value it is quintessentially South African. Told originally
by a South African to his own children (who were later taken by
ox-wagon to visit the original scenes of his adventures), it describes his adventures in the Eastern Transvaal with none of the
clumsy didactic digressions on flora, fauna and native life that ear-

lier writers used to include for their European readers. FitzPatrick's biographer, A.P. Cartwright, named him, in the title of his
biography, *The First South African*. The quality of the prose, the
vigour, self-confidence and grand scale of *Jock of the Bushveld*,
remain unmatched to this day. Not only is the book regularly reprinted, but edited, condensed, simplified and bowdlerised versions
continue to be published – the latest being Irma Holland's version,
A Bushveld Story (1987); and it is still in use as a class reader in
some schools, as well as being a popular library book among Std 5
and 6 pupils.

Yet in spite of the novel indigenous quality of *Jock*, FitzPatrick
was a man of his time and his book reflects typical colonial attitudes. He was born in South Africa but, as was customary for
those who could afford it, was sent to England for his secondary
education. He fully supported Britain against the Transvaal Republic, receiving in turn imprisonment and a fine from the Republic
for his part in the Jameson Raid and a knighthood for services to
Britain during the Anglo-Boer War. Although he later endorsed
game conservation, in *Jock* there is almost no questioning of the
shooting of wild creatures, and the values which he propagates are
those of Victorian imperialism, as Stephen Gray has pointed out:

> *FitzPatrick's animal biography is told as a historical docu-
> mentary which describes the 'old life' of the pre- industrial
> wilderness to a new generation, to whom the pioneering
> ideals of loyalty, athleticism, sportsmanship and the proce-
> dures for domesticating nature are becoming lost. The
> readers of the 'new life' are thus addressed in cautionary
> terms and with a didactic purpose, and* Jock of the
> Bushveld *is devised to reactivate in the present the youth-
> ful virtues of obedience, self-reliance, adventurousness and
> common sense which FitzPatrick sees as having epitomised
> the arrival of the European spirit in Africa.*[8]

The essentially British nature of education in South Africa continued well into the twentieth century. Evidence points to World War
II as marking the change to a new South Africanism. Until 1942,
for example, the Transvaal Education Department prescribed *two*
histories of English literature among the nine prescribed works for
Senior Certificate English First Language. In 1943 only one was

prescribed, and that was dropped the following year, never to reappear. The most significant support for the thesis that the mid-century saw the switch of English-speaking South Africans from a British to an indigenous model for their language and culture is provided by the linguistic research of L.W. Lanham. In earlier years, he says,

> *a feature of British 'top-dog' attitudes practised in the society was the denigration of what was obviously local and the ascription of quality and excellence to what was British. This extended to the 'colonial', who was rated socially inferior to those who were 'home-born'. Home-born mothers admonished their children with 'you little colonial' at least until the 1930s.*
>
> *Social types perceived and labelled in the society were: British, Colonial, Dutch. We have a report of this distinction being applied in a major South African industry as late as the 1940s.*[9]

In another study Lanham states:

> *The linguistic evidence indicates that the change in English-speaking society came immediately after the last war and it takes the form of a great dilution of urban, nineteenth century British English by the main stream of rural, local South African English. I believe that this must have coincided with one pattern of social values and attitudes giving place to another.*[10]

Lanham ascribes this change to the disappearance of a reference group of expatriate 'distinguished headmasters' and 'upper-class Englishmen from positions of social power and influence in the English cities'.

Further evidence of the cultural shift is that adult South African English literature also changed at this time. This is confirmed by Van Wyk Smith in his historical survey, *Grounds of Contest*: '… at last, after the Second World War, a more distinctively South African accent became audible in our literature…'[11] Heale also marks the mid-century as a turning point for children's literature: 'For at least the first half of this century, English-speaking children in

South Africa relied on books published in England,'[12] whereafter indigenous books started to appear. The trend is also visible in the publication of popular non-fiction. In pre-war years, the yarns of country life by Leonard Flemming (*Fool on the Veld* [1916], *The Call of the Veld* [1924], etc) and Kingsley Fairbridge (The Story of *Kingsley Fairbridge by Himself* [1927]) had already been popular. Then, in the 1950s, there was such a spate of books by T.V. Bulpin, Lawrence Green and others about old South Africa that it must be evidence of a huge upsurge of interest in tales of pioneers in wild country.

The end of the war brought further urbanisation of English speakers, the beginnings of political distancing from Britain, and the return of soldiers from abroad, where their encounter with Europe emphasised their otherness. With these changes came a search to find a South African character for education. The result was that English teaching and what little children's book publishing there was, turned to rural South Africa for material – inevitably, a country life of hunting and farming. This espousal of the rural past as the authentic culture of English-speaking South Africans was in many ways false. The reality is that apart from a few farmers they have always been urban people. Most British immigrants were white-collar workers or urban craftsmen and traders who soon congregated in towns. Rapid urbanisation after the war left only about five per cent of English-speakers living in villages or on farms by the 1970s.[13] The South African English language that was now becoming acceptable reflects this: William Branford, one of the team who worked on the *Dictionary of South African English*, reported that in their initial corpus – of 1 100 items – about half the abstract nouns were political: *Afrikanerdom, verkramptheid, apartheid, baasskap, job reservation, kragdadigheid*, etc; and in the category of non-living concrete nouns,

> there is a strong preponderance of items reflecting material culture: less involvement, as one might expect, with fountain, berg and sweetveld, than with barberton, bottle store, minedump and national road.[14]

However, the stereotype of South African English culture ignored this modernity. It is typified by what Branford calls the English of the Van der Merwe story. When in 1970 he invited readers of

Personality magazine to send him typical South African English words, he found that the words they submitted could only generate sentences such as, 'Ag ja but it was lekker koeksusters by Tannie's braaivleis,' and 'Eina Marie, there's a gogga in my veldskoen.'[15]

Typical of this post-war fixation on the rural past, from the 1930s right up until 1959 the Transvaal Education Department English syllabuses gave, as a topic for oral composition, 'How to make butter'. Until the 1970s English text books and examination papers contained few comprehension passages with a South African theme, and those that did were either wild life adventures or glimpses of nineteenth century tribal life in the form of visits by white men to 'native kraals'. There was little in English teaching that dealt with technological matters – text books, comprehension tests and composition topics ignored the subject until the 1970s.[16]

A typical school reader was *Tales of Veld and Vlei: for Junior High Schools*, edited by J.P. Coetzer, which was published in 1964 and ran to many impressions. It contained thirty short pieces of writing of about two to three pages each, most of which are devoid of literary merit, many by anonymous authors. Apart from stories by Pauline Smith and Herman Charles Bosman, the passages were mainly anecdotes about wild animals, Voortrekkers, Eastern Cape Frontier Wars, the Anglo-Boer War and the Mfecane. As late as 1974 Purnell published in its ELISA Series (English Literature in South Africa) an anthology edited by Geoffrey Haresnape, entitled *The Great Hunters*, which was intended for 'senior pupils and students'. Although the readings included many passages describing gory wholesale slaughter of game, trophy hunting and pointless shooting of individual animals, they were presented for the most part uncritically, the emphasis being on their intrinsic interest and the background notes on the authors.

So obsessed with hunting adventures and sketches of native life were the education authorities that in 1947 the Transvaal Education Department prescribed for the Senior Certificate an American nineteenth century traveller's narrative, Francis Parkman's *The Oregon Trail: Sketches of Prairie and Rocky-Mountain Life*. First published in 1849, it was an American classic, relatively unknown outside the USA, describing Parkman's expedition of 1846 in which he lived among the Indians and participated in buffalo hunts – the counterpart of the narratives of his contemporaries in Africa. The only reason this obscure book on frontier life could possibly have been selected as a matriculation setwork is that educationists considered its subject matter appropriate for South African children. It is no coincidence that the first novel by a South African to be prescribed by the Transvaal Education Department is subtitled 'A Bushveld Story'. This was *Out of the Strong* by R. Lighton, prescribed in 1961. It had been preceded by only one novel with an African flavour, John Buchan's *Prester John*, in 1956. The Education Department had wasted little time waiting to see if it would be established in the canon of respected South African literature, for it had been published only four years previously. Described in a contemporary review in the *Pretoria News* as a 'South African novel which never once mentions race',[17] it is a typical *plaasroman* about the intrigues of white farmers and country shoolmasters. The following year *Cattle thief: The story of Ntsukumbini*, by Frank Brownlee, was prescribed, after which no South African novels were prescribed for another ten years. Jonathan Paton remarks that 'It would be fair to say that these writers are virtually unheard of today and even in the 1950s and 1960s were obscure.'[18] But for the Education Department they were South African, and they were 'safe'.

The classic example of the increasing interest in hunting and animal adventures is the popularity of Victor Pohl's *Bushveld Adventures*, published in 1940. This is a book of reminiscences of his early life, mostly concerning hunting adventures and encounters with animals, told in a flat, awkward style. (Pohl was actually Afrikaans-speaking.) *Bushveld Adventures* became extraordinarily successful and it was actually prescribed by the Transvaal as a non-fiction setwork for English First Language in the Senior Certificate in 1946, ran through numerous editions, and in 1972 was still the most frequent source of passages for comprehension tests in the Std 8 internal examinations set by teachers of English as First Language in Transvaal Education Department schools. This book was a key text in the back-to-the-Bushveld movement after the War. It has a pivotal position since it looks back to *Jock of the Bushveld*, which unquestioningly accepted unlimited hunting, yet also presages modern children's books, which promote environmental conservation. Because of the significance of *Bushveld Adventures*, I examine it closely later in this chapter before moving on in the next chapter to discuss children's books with an environmental theme.

Interest in the Lowveld of the Eastern Transvaal had been sustained in the first half of the twentieth century not only by the constant popularity of *Jock of the Bushveld* but also by the development of what finally became in 1926 the Kruger National Park, and the publication of a few books that glamourised its pioneer game rangers. By the 1940s, hunting stories had to compete with children's books that specifically promoted the concept of 'game sanctuaries' – a simple, rather mystical, view of conservation that did not take into account the complexities of ecological interdependence that are the concern of modern environmental conservation and are reflected in modern children's fiction on this theme. Between 1938 and 1941 the United Tobacco Company ('Manufacturers of "C to C" Cigarettes') brought out a popular series of cigarette cards with handsome albums to match, on the themes of 'Our South African Flora', 'Our South African Birds', 'Our South Africa Past and Present' and 'Our South African National Parks'. The texts were by distinguished authorities – Dr Austin Roberts edited the Bird volume and Col. Stevenson-Hamilton wrote the text on National Parks. Although the tobacconist publishers announced on the title pages that the project was 'for the benefit of smokers of their products', in all likelihood it was children who collected and pasted in the attractive cards and read the captions and snatches of the texts.

Another writer who promoted conservation was C.S. Stokes, who wrote *Sanctuary* and *We're Telling You* (1943), a book of verse for children in which wild animals speak about themselves. In an odd marriage, his two books were sold for War Funds, and the verse makes several references to the current war, as well as rather incongruously applying wartime imagery such as 'blitzkrieg', 'searchlights', 'bombs', and 'Uncle Bill' to nature. *We're Telling You* is a jolly book, celebrating the creation of sanctuaries. Some of the illustrations are comic, to match the comic verse, while others are beautiful naturalistic animal studies by the well-known wild life artist C.T. Astley Maberly which enhance the serious message of the book. Whether children would actually read or enjoy it is a moot point: the Foreword to the second edition by Mrs Isie Smuts and the other tributes reprinted there suggest that it appealed to adults. It is just a pity that the verse is so bad. This is a superior example:

*The rhino cleared his throat, as chairmen are inclined to
do,
And then addressed the odd-assorted folk of Nature's zoo;
I speak, of course, from long and ripe experience (he said),
For since my cradle days, my friends, a hundred years
have sped.
In mind, I look back down the years, and see blood every-
where –
I see it dye our homelands, and I smell it in the air,
And beasts writhe in their torture, in the main the sadist's
prey,
For manglings of creatures made 'a sportsman's holiday'*

*Stark fear was mine through youngsterhood, maturing
years, and prime,
For whining, rending bullets seemed to haunt me all the
time,
But man has said good-bye to that, and so I bow my head
In gratitude that where he killed, he now protects instead.*

Contrived and 'precious' as *We're Telling You* may appear to us
today, it was not *sui generis*, for it resembles in many ways a
contemporary series of South African children's books that was
extremely popular – the 'Cock-Olly' books of May Henderson.
The first in this series was *The Cock-Olly Book: Tales of Veld, Fun
and Frolic*, published in Durban in 1941. It was soon followed by
three sequels, presumably in response to popular demand: *Looma,
Teller of Tales: More Stories of Kruger Park* (1943), *Tortoo the
Tortoise: Ruler of Kruger Park* (1943) and *Mrs Mouse of Kruger
Park* (1944), by which time *Cock-Olly* and *Looma* were in their
fourth printing. Considering the restrictions on printing during the
war years, the frequent reprints of these books and *We're Telling
You* attest to their popularity. A review quoted on the cover of *Mrs
Mouse* says that 'The animals in the Cock-Olly books are probably
the best-known and best-loved animals in South African children's
literature.' The stories are aimed at young children, with comic
illustrations to match, reminiscent of those in *We're Telling You*.
They are lively stories, packed with dialogue, action, and verse,
about a group of anthropomorphised creatures, including very
small ones such as termites.

At one point in *Looma* a squad of soldiers inexplicably marches smartly through the Kruger Park, watched admiringly by the animals. Bearing in mind the war connections of *We're Telling You*, it is not surprising to find that *Looma* also had an Introduction by 'Mrs J.C. Smuts ("Ouma")', and that the books were sold in aid of the Air Raid Heroes Fund. Today we forget that South African soldiers of World War II were known universally as the 'Springboks': the connection between the Kruger National Park game sanctuary and South African patriotism ran deep.

Another genre of children's books which may be seen as a product of the 'Bushveld Syndrome' is the collection of South African folktales. The whole enterprise of publishing English and Afrikaans children's versions of African folktales may be seen as part of this inclination to publish books about the rural past, as we have seen in Chapter One.

When I drew attention in 1977 to the post-war phenomenon of the upsurge of interest in the rural past, I called it the 'Bushveld Syndrome in South African English teaching'.[19] Unbeknown to me, Patricia McMagh had already coined the term 'Bushveld-Wildebees-Complex' in 1967, to describe one aspect of the same phenomenon, namely, the registers of English language taught in schools:

> *If our second language teaching is to be directed towards equipping people to USE English, in the South African urbanized setting, we will be able to discard our preoccupation with the bushveld-wildebees-complex – the approach which has persisted for so long in teaching the kind of English that would be currency between nomadic hunters, or equip its students to become professional safari organizers.*[20]

The English of the 'Bushveld-wildebees-complex' is the product of the ethos of the entire English curriculum – literature, comprehension passages, grammar exercises, vocabulary, idiomatic language, and writing and speech topics.

Literary critics have coined other pejorative terms to describe the Bushveld Syndrome as it is manifested in adult South African English literature, where the strain persists to this day. Larson identifies the 'nostalgic-pastoral' type of novel;[21] and Richard

Rive speaks of 'veld and vlei' writing:

> *The best [white writers] have extended themselves to inter-*
> *national themes, though still rooted in the South African*
> *experience. The worst are either writing escapistically or*
> *producing 'veld and vlei' prose and verse.*[22]

The term 'veld and vlei' is also used by Malvern van Wyk Smith[23] and Jonathan Paton with the same connotation.[24]

There are perhaps four explanations of this 'syndrome'. The first is that educators genuinely could not see anything authentically South African in the modern urban environment, and therefore felt they had to turn to the Bushveld to give English teaching an indigenous flavour.

Secondly, the parallel situation in Afrikaans teaching was that all the prescribed works had a South African setting, one that was almost invariably the rural past – animal stories for the primary school, and *plaasromans*, *Trekkerromans*, and hunting stories by Sangiro for the high school. To be 'South African' therefore meant ransacking available South African English writing for anything suitable, since works in genres comparable to the Afrikaans ones were scarce. A.C. Partridge's reader for school pupils, *Readings in South African English Prose* (1948), which was often prescribed, epitomises this enterprise: it has sections on The Country, The People, Domestic Life, Historical and Other Sketches, Letters, Biography and Reminiscences, Nature, Native Sketches, Short Stories, Essays, Criticism, and Philosophy and Religion. All the well-known writers usually included in early attempts to establish a South African canon were there, among them Lady Anne Barnard, Thomas Pringle, Olive Schreiner, Pauline Smith, Kingsley Fairbridge, Leonard Flemming, Sarah Gertrude Millin, Percy FitzPatrick, and Frank Brownlee, with the surprising addition of Jan Smuts and R.F.A. Hoernlé – making a bulky volume, indigestible to school pupils. (I speak with feeling, as one who had to read it as a fifteen-year-old, when it was prescribed by the Natal Education Department.)

The third explanation for the Bushveld Syndrome is that the hunter, farmer and game ranger represented a set of values which, although they were degenerate derivatives of Victorian values, were still admired. Lanham explains:

Those in the South African English community who give allegiance to the 'South African tradition' in social values find attractive the 'local man' identity and the values which it represents: self-reliance, strong local loyalties, masculine and physical toughness, gregariousness, in-group cohesion and conformity.[25]

Research which Vivian de Klerk completed in 1989 into the language of English-speaking high school pupils as an index of social values in government and private schools showed that these values are still promoted in South Africa. She found, for instance, that 'the hidden curriculum favours males, not females, in co-educational environments':

Sex-related linguistic differences do exist ... These differences have been shown to relate to the social factors of power and status: males show clear signs of being more confident, assertive, relaxed, unworried and unhurried ... Females generally, and government school pupils (versus private school pupils) are the less 'privileged' groups, and display concomitant linguistic behaviour which suggests the socialisation patterns which produced it: more restrictions and conformity to sex-typed patterns of behaviour.[26]

The degenerate version of these 'masculine' values and their brutal consequences, to be found in both fictional and real schools in the 1990s, are described in Chapter Six. In contrast, we shall see later that modern South African youth literature which has an environmental theme does not promote the manly values associated with the Bushveld Syndrome.

The fourth explanation for the Syndrome is that there was a nostalgia for the somewhat mythical, innocent, rural past. This accords with F. Davis's theory about the prevalence of nostalgia in the West in the late twentieth century. He argues that nostalgia compensates for feelings of dislocation and discontinuity (such as those occasioned by the upheavals of World War II), and that its typical modern manifestation is a yearning for the rural past as a reaction against technology.[27] How apt his theory is for South Africa is well illustrated by the case of A.C. Partridge. In 1969, twenty-one years after his *Readings in South African English*

Prose appeared, he published a new prose anthology, entitled *Scenes from South African Life*, 'for the discriminating reader and students at schools or universities'. So committed was he to his enterprise of keeping the past alive that he included an appeal for 'suggestions for future volumes'. The words of his Preface reflect his response to the changes that had occurred in South Africa since the war. In all seriousness he concludes:

> *Those who had the good fortune to be born in a colonial Arcadia, and to survive the grotesque realities of the post-war economic revolution, may read certain pages with a lingering regret. But the changes that oppress the city-dweller have not yet deprived him of a hinterland of typical African tranquility. It is to be hoped that these scenes will recompense the patriot by refreshing him in memory and spirit.*

> *Hence, in a season of calm weather*
> *Though inland far we be,*
> *Our souls have sight of that immortal sea*
> *Which brought us hither,*
> *Can in a moment travel thither –*
> *And see the children sport upon the shore.*[28]

Four years later Partridge published a collection of folktales entitled *Folklore of Southern Africa*. His self-confessed nostalgia for a 'colonial Arcadia' is a further indication that for some people, publishing South African folktales was motivated by nostalgia.

There are of course English-speaking South Africans for whom the nostalgia takes the form of longing for the British rather than South African past. Branford remarks that some people react negatively to the stereotyped rural image of South African culture by regarding it as something primitive: they find South African English 'informal if not positively crude'.[29] In the writings of white English-speaking children in the late 1970s there were still to be found idealised images of a chocolate-box cover, bucolic England derived, presumably, from kitsch images still current in their culture: a land of twittering robins, squirrels, and 'shepherds weather-worn in wind and snow'.[30] Children's reading reinforces their British ties, for there are still relatively few South African books to fill their school prescribed lists or leisure hours.

Consequently, the Bushveld trend has always been counterbalanced by an absurdly British element. In 1953, for example, the Cape Education Department prescribed two insignificant but quintessentially English novels, *Berry and Co* by Dornford Yates for the Std 7s, and *The Small House at Allington* by Anthony Trollope (alongside Pauline Smith's *The Little Karoo*) for the Senior Certificate. Marguerite Poland gives a poignant vignette in *Shadow of the Wild Hare* of the little girl Rosie, who lives on a farm in the Eastern Cape, reading in bed a story about English stable girls and ponies while she herself is engaged in a tense and mysterious adventure involving an African medicine man. In similar vein, I remember how my brother and I, as wild little farm boys in 1950 (very much, I'm afraid, like Rendall's Children of the Sun), would take shelter from the blazing sun in the Khomas Hochland mountains of South West Africa by lying on our beds in the daghawalled farmhouse, reading our favourite author – Arthur Ransome.

The disorientation which English speakers felt after the war became exacerbated by political developments in subsequent years. As the possibility of regaining political power from the Afrikaner became increasingly remote, and at the same time it became apparent that the real political issues of the country now concerned relations between black and white rather than between English and Afrikaner, the English speakers tried to define their identity and mark out their future. Historians sought out and recounted with pride the contribution that the English had made in South Africa, producing books with markedly assertive titles: A.P. Cartwright's *The First South African*, John Bond's *They Were South Africans*, F.C. Metrowich's *The Valiant But Once*, A.M. Lewin Robinson's *None Daring to Make Us Afraid*, Guy Butler's *When Boys Were Men*, Celia Sadler's *Never a Young Man*, R.M. de Villiers's *Better Than They Knew*.

The culmination, and in a way the end of this movement, came in 1974, the year in which the 1820 Settlers National Monument was opened in Grahamstown, but also the year in which, at the 'Poetry 74' conference in Cape Town, Mike Kirkwood launched his now celebrated attack on what he called 'Butlerism' – 'the contradiction between the long view of history and a romantic, nostalgic identification with a partial aspect'.[31] Since then, almost unnoticed, English speakers have dropped their self-conscious search for a place in South Africa. They have, without deliberate effort, 'taken root', as Guy Butler had exhorted them to when he entitled his play *Take Root or Die*, paraphrasing the 1820 settler H.H. Dugmore.

Those same areas in education and cultural life which in the past evinced either the Bushveld Syndrome or a clinging to things British, today reflect contemporary South Africa. J.M. Coetzee's novels *Dusklands* and *In the Heart of the Country* have effectively deconstructed the nostalgic-pastoral tradition of South African novels. School syllabuses, teaching materials and examination papers incorporate South African writers and subject matter, and in the 1970s and 1980s an increasing number of English language children's writers have been able to find local publishers and a market for their fiction and non-fiction. Among the juvenile novels of these two decades a theme has emerged which deals with the South African countryside and its flora and fauna in a very different way to the books of the past that had glorified hunting and the manly qualities of the hunters, or limited the concept of conservation to the creation of game sanctuaries. This modern theme is environmental conservation, and there are about two dozen books on the subject which I discuss in the next chapter. Since they are the heirs to a tradition of writing about the wild life of Southern Africa that goes back well over two hundred years, they cannot be considered in isolation, and we have to step back for a moment to see where the shift occurred in children's books from a hunting to a conservation ethic.

The reasons given in nineteenth century books for the shooting of wild creatures are blurred. Missionaries describe how they shot for the pot. Naturalists shot for specimens. Sportsmen also shot for the sake of science or the pot, as well as for their main purposes, which were for fun and for trophy hunting. Everybody, not only the traders, appears to have hunted for profit. Even 'shooting for the pot' becomes a problematic reason for hunting when it comes to feeding local inhabitants, as we shall see from the case of Victor Pohl. The great hunt of Prince Alfred, in which 600 head of large game were killed in one day, was simply an exaggerated confirmation of what the hunters' books had been indicating all along, namely that a lot of shooting was done out of sheer bloodthirstiness. In all this slaughter, there are only occasional hints of ambivalence, where a writer pauses to admire his prey, or expresses a fear that the wild life is being exterminated. Nor must it be thought that all the hunters were Europeans, simply visiting southern Africa to use it as a playground or to plunder it. True, the great names were Selous, Cornwallis Harris and Gordon Cumming, but the fact is that since the seventeenth century the wild life had been systematically exploited for commercial purposes by the residents. In Namibia, practically all the wild life was shot out in the nineteenth century mainly by the Oorlam, to meet the demands of traders from the Cape,[32] and the same was happening south of the Orange. South Africa had many Boer commercial hunters. For example, Haresnape identifies Pieter Jacobs (1800-1882) as

> *perhaps the greatest of the many Boer hunters. [He] started hunting in the African interior in the 1840s, and continued until about 1880. He killed between 400 and 500 bull elephants …Died as a result of injuries received when mauled by a lion.*[33]

At the beginning of the twentieth century the age of uninhibited hunting was drawing to an end. Percy FitzPatrick, whose own hunting days had ended long before *Jock* was published, espoused the cause of control over hunting and poaching. Gradually the conservation ethic began to receive popular acceptance, and by the mid-twentieth century even hunters had to pay lip-service to it. This was, as we have seen, a time of revaluation and reorientation. Victor Pohl, who had been born an Afrikaner and actually imprisoned in a British Boer War prisoner-of-war camp when a young boy, wrote in English the history of his pioneer family, *Land of Distant Horizons* (1946), and later a well-known novel, *Farewell the Little People* (1968), which honoured the memory of the exterminated San. In his *Bushveld Adventures* we can see enacted the ambivalence of the change of heart about hunting.

The conditions under which Pohl had roamed free, shooting at will, first as a boy on the Eastern Free State/Basutoland border before the Anglo-Boer War, and later, in 1914/15, as a young man in the Eastern Transvaal and Portuguese East Africa, had long since disappeared when he published his memories of those times in 1940. He himself had, like FitzPatrick, subsequently changed his attitude towards hunting, and his later works show his concern for conservation of the unspoilt past. Yet in spite of his disclaimers, the actual text of his book contains contradictions that betray the complexity of the moral issues of hunting.

A theme of the book is embodied in his statement that, except for some big game shot under licence for trading purposes, 'We never shot except for food or safety' (123). This is endorsed by Deneys Reitz in his Foreword:

> *Though he lives in a land of hereditary hunters he never shoots for the mere sport of killing, but prefers to follow game and other wild animals to their own haunts, there to study them at first hand and to write of them as a friend and protector.*

In fact, there is less overt didacticism about nature or description of wild life in *Bushveld Adventures* than in the writings of FitzPatrick or his predecessors; but what little naturalist content there is, Pohl admits he took partly from Stevenson-Hamilton's *Animal Life in Africa* (81).

In order to consider the claim that he shot only 'for the pot' we can begin by examining the terminology that he uses to refer to his prey. Like many of the earlier hunters, he is fond of using elegant variation when referring to the creatures, in order to avoid repetition: a crocodile becomes 'the saurian', a lion predictably is called 'the king of the beasts' and a leopard becomes a 'carnivorous beast'. However, the terms often anthropomorphise the wild creatures, giving them unsavoury human qualities which accordingly imply justification for their death. Early in the book a hawk at which the boys take pot shots is casually referred to as 'the murderer' without explanation. Crocodiles are called 'brutes', which is also the term commonly applied by hunters to their prey in the works excerpted in Coetzer's school reader, *Tales of Veld and Vlei* – it suggests viciousness in the animal, and implies that the hunter resents the animals' dogged resistance to death. Just because leopards attack baboons – their natural prey – he calls them 'marauders' and 'spotted terrors'. Baboons in turn are 'dangerous and treacherous', and the 'devil incarnate'. Hyenas are 'loathsome' and mambas 'degraded'. When he describes how his party hunted down a pack of wild dogs, one by one, until they were all killed, the anthropomorphism is so strong that all one has to do is apply his terminology to the men and the tables are turned – the dogs, after all, were hunting for food, but the men, he confesses, 'were out for blood': 'The killers ... The hateful dogs, those merciless and remorseless hunters that strike greater terror into animals than any other beast of prey' (121). We can conclude that a good proportion of the creatures he shot were not antelope, and that his reasons for killing them had sinister origins in his subconscious.

Besides shooting the wild dogs, he and his brother often hunted for sport. For example, the very first bushveld adventure that he describes is a lion hunt for which no explanation is advanced. They also shot leopards and at one point he mentions in passing, 'I caught a glimpse of the swish of a lone sable bull's tail – the very animal we wanted, as none of the party had as yet procured one' (52). (After firing, he assumes he 'only slightly wounded it', for it got away.)

Pohl emphasises that they observed a strict ethical code in their hunting. They followed 'established principles' of not shooting cows or immature animals 'even for food', and never letting a wounded animal go if at all possible. A paradoxical aspect of his hunting, which is to be found in the writings of most South African hunters, is that every now and then he admires the animals, remarking, for example, that kudu are 'powerful and beautiful'.[34]

The ontology of hunting is far more complex than Pohl imagines. He gives several reasons why they shot animals. Apart from shooting for the pot they hunted predators that were killing local blacks and their livestock, and they shot big game under licence to recoup the expenses of their expedition – though they were so sickened at shooting an elephant that they did not repeat it. Astonishingly, after acknowledging that the 'white man's rifle' was exterminating antelope, he justifies shooting lions by saying that in doing so 'the principal slayer of the antelope is also kept in check' (33). He argues:

From the first trek to the last, our enjoyment of the freedom of the open spaces and the adventures they offered was in no way dependent on the slaughtering of animals, and we had never shot except for food or safety. (123)

But even his excuse that they were shooting essential food is spurious. After all, if they had not been in the bushveld in the first place, they would have been eating normal food produced on a farm or bought from shops, and they would not have been shooting hippopotamuses 'as a necessary aid to defray expenses' (124).

The gap between what Pohl claims to be saying about hunting in the book and what he actually says would appear to be partly a genuine blindness on his part; but when Deneys Reitz contributes a foreword in which he tells the reader to read what is simply not there, one must conclude that the two of them are forming a conspiracy with the reader to assuage their consciences of the guilt of enjoying the hunting stories. Pohl's attitude towards hunting had really changed little from that of nineteenth century hunters or that of FitzPatrick.

Apart from shooting the wildlife, their expeditions also interacted with the local black inhabitants, some of whom they employed temporarily, and many of whom enjoyed eating the meat that the shooting provided. Pohl's references to these people involve little reflection. There is something ironic in the freedom of the white man to roam, shooting at will, while – as he points out – the inhabitants are barred from setting snares. 'One need not fear for the extermination of the antelope by these primitive folk', he remarks patronisingly (33).

Stephen Gray has exposed the fallacy of hunters' arguing that it was a part of the white man's burden that they had to shoot to provide meat for their servants: if the hunters hadn't employed them, thereby taking them away from their homes, they would not have had to be fed.[35] Pohl records an anecdote that shows how the hunters had disturbed the normal way of life of the local inhabitants. After his servant had expertly caught a squirrel, almost as a reflex action,

> *in the ordinary course of events that squirrel would have served as part of his evening meal and been relished as such, but now that he was hunting in the company of his white masters he merely gave the carcass a contemptuous look before he flung it away. (62)*

Pohl makes no comment upon this easy adoption of the 'white masters'' behaviour. In fact, he seems unaware of the central paradox of the explorer and, for that matter, the tourist – a paradox well known in quantum physics and the philosophy of science: the presence of an observer alters the nature of the observed phenomenon. The explorer and the tourist desire to be the only stranger present in the alien environment, but by their presence they render it no longer alien. The romantic traveller wishes to be alone with unspoilt nature, but his or her presence, by definition, spoils it. The practical consequences are all too well known to the authorities who have to protect tourist spots and wilderness areas from the damage caused by visitors seeking solitude. Pohl, like many earlier travellers in Africa, but with a new sense of urgency, found its open spaces an escape from the civilized world:

> Little did I think as I gazed over those untravelled wilds how Eric and I were destined to roam them in years to come, and how the glorious sense of freedom that we would experience in those vast solitudes would grip our very souls and impart an indefinable restlessness of spirit that would always rebel against the petty tyrannies and the empty vanities of the civilized order. (16)

Yet he apparently did not realise that he was not only destroying the solitude but also contributing to the permanent destruction of the wilds that he himself deplored and described so feelingly in his Preface to *Farewell the Little People*: '... most of the natural beauties of our land have been to a greater or less extent marred by the inroads of civilization, ... touched by the desecrating hand of modern man.'[36] No writer at the end of the twentieth century can display the same naivety. The children's writers of the 1980s to whom we turn in the next chapter acknowledge that human beings are part of the ecology of the entire country, and they explore our moral and spiritual response to this oneness.

NOTES

1. J.A. Mangan, *The Games Ethic and Imperialism*, Harmondsworth: Viking, 1986, 117.
2. J.R. de S. Honey, 'Arnolds of the bushveld,' *Symposium*, 1975/76, 25.
3. G.M.H. Bobbins, *The Twilight of English*, Cape Town: Maskew Miller, 1951.

4. Montague J. Rendall, quoted in Mangan, *The Games Ethic, 31*.
5. M. van Wyk Smith, *Grounds of Contest*, Cape Town: Juta & Co, 1990, 68.
6. David Adey, Ridley Beeton, Michael Chapman, Ernest Pereira, *Companion to South African English Literature*, Johannesburg: Ad Donker, 1986, 51.
7. Jay Heale, 'South African children's books in English,' in *Doer-Land-y/Far Far Away*, ed. Marianne Hölscher, Cape Town: South African National Gallery, 1986, 12.
8. Stephen Gray, 'Domesticating the wilds: J. Percy FitzPatrick's *Jock of the Bushveld* as a historical record for children,' *English in Africa*, 14:2, October 1987, 1.
9. L.W. Lanham and C.A. Macdonald, *The Standard in South African English and its Social History*, Amsterdam: Groos, 1979, 76.
10. L.W. Lanham, 'South African English as an index of social history,' *English Studies in Africa*, 13:1, March 1970, 263.
11. M. van Wyk Smith, *Grounds of Contest*, i.
12. Heale, 'South African children's books in English', 11.
13. H.L. Watts, 'A social and demographic portrait of English-speaking white South Africans,' in *English-speaking South Africa Today*, ed. Andre de Villiers, Oxford: Oxford University Press, 1976, 52.
14. William Branford, 'A Dictionary of South African English as a reflex of the English-speaking cultures of South Africa,' in *English-speaking South Africa Today*, 308 and 309.
15. Branford, 'A Dictonary of South African English', 298.
16. Elwyn Jenkins, 'The nature of English Higher as a secondary school subject in the Transvaal, 1942-1972,' unpublished MEd dissertation, Johannesburg: University of the Witwatersrand, 1973.
17. John Tucker, 'South African novel which never once mentions race,' *Pretoria News*, 7 January 1957.
18. Jonathan Paton, 'English and the teaching of English literature in South Africa,' in *Teaching and Learning English Worldwide*, ed. James Britton, Robert E. Shafer and Ken Watson, Clevedon, Philadelphia: Multilingual Matters, 1990, 244.
19. Elwyn Jenkins, 'The bushveld syndrome in South African English teaching,' *CRUX*, 11:4, October 1977, 17.
20. Patricia McMagh, 'What are we going to teach? And how?' *CRUX*, 4:7, August 1967, 47.
21. C.R. Larson, *The Emergence of African Fiction*, Bloomington: Indiana Press, 1972.

22. Richard Rive, 'The black writer and South African literature,' in *Towards Understanding/Op Weg na Begrip*, ed. Isabel Cilliers, Cape Town: Maskew Miller Longman, 1988, 209.

23. M. van Wyk Smith, *Grounds of Contest,* i.

24. Jonathan Paton, 'English and the teaching of English literature', 243.

25. Lanham and Macdonald, *The Standard in South African English, 83.*

26. Vivian de Klerk, 'An investigation into the language of English-speaking adolescents, with particular reference to sex, age and type of school,' unpublished PhD thesis, Cape Town: University of Cape Town, 1989, 193.

27. F. Davis, *Yearning for Yesterday: a Sociology of Nostalgia*, New York: The Free Press, 1979.

28. A.C. Partridge, *Scenes from South African Life*, London: Evans Brothers, 1969, ix.

29. Branford, 'A Dictionary of South African English', 298.

30. Elwyn Jenkins, 'Our teenagers are romantics,' *Transvaal Educational News*, 78:7, August 1981, 15.

31. Mike Kirkwood, 'The colonizer: a critique of the English South African culture theory,' in *Poetry South Africa: Selected Papers from Poetry 74*, ed. P. Wilhelm and J. Polley, Johannesburg: Ad Donker, 1976, 104.

32. Brigitte Lau, *Namibia in Jonker Afrikaner's Time*, Windhoek: National Archives, 1987.

33. Geoffrey Haresnape, ed. *The Great Hunters*, Cape Town: Purnell, 1974, 72.

34. The same point is made about nineteenth century travellers such as Thomas Baines by Dorian Haarhoff, *The Wild South-West: Frontier Myths and Metaphors in Literature set in Namibia, 1760-1988*, Johannesburg: Witwatersrand University Press, 1991, 37.

35. Stephen Gray, *Southern African Literature: an Introduction*, Cape Town: David Philip, 1979, 105.

36. Victor Pohl, *Farewell, the Little People*, Cape Town: Oxford University Press, 1968, i.

CHAPTER FOUR

The Environment

Children's fiction as a response to environmental issues

South Africans have in the past had a limited understanding of what conservation entails. The saga of the Kruger National Park, begun in 1898 and finally consolidated under its present name in 1926, focussed popular attention for many years on the creation of inland game sanctuaries, and it was primarily the survival of large mammals that caught the popular imagination. When Stevenson-Hamilton's cigarette-card album appeared in 1940 there were only five national parks – Kruger, Addo, Kalahari, Bredasdorp, Bontebok and Mountain Zebra. His use of the term 'sanctuary' is significant as it implies that the main intention was to protect animals from extinction.[1] C.S. Stokes's immensely popular book on the reserves, published in 1944, had the same word for its title, *Sanctuary*; and Stevenson-Hamilton entitled his history of the Kruger Park *South African Eden*. Their choice of these words has religious undertones. Not only was the preservation of the animals a sacred trust, but there is an element of pantheism in the motivation of conservationists of that time.

However, just as hunting was a more complex activity than writers such as Pohl made out, so modern society has a far wider perception of conservation – a perception that blurs forever the old dichotomy between town and country which was part of the

Bushveld Syndrome. For it is now understood that all parts of the country, all sections of the population, and all aspects of modern civilization are involved in environmental issues. It has become apparent that it is a fallacy to think that creating game reserves leaves areas of the country unspoilt, and that resources can exist without reference to their geographical and human context. The balance of nature has been everywhere disturbed and now requires constant human intervention to maintain equilibrium.

Brian Huntley, Director of the Botanical Research Institute, puts it this way:

> *South African conservationists must now tear themselves away from their indulgence in non-issues such as rhinos and elephants. No longer is it sufficient to claim that these are important flagship species – symbols of greater needs. We are going to have to make environmentalism relevant to the new players in South Africa's future – the disenfranchised majority that will shortly be placing a completely new array of demands on South Africa's resources.*[2]

Today, environmental education finds a place in school science syllabuses. But it is not simply science that is needed to cope with environmental issues. Environmental conservation has ethical, moral and aesthetic components. A.J. Clacherty's 1988 thesis on environmental education in South Africa concluded that 'the solution to the problem of environmental degradation lies in the people: their perceptions, attitudes, values and behaviour in relation to their environment'.[3] Ian Player, the Natal conservationist, believes that the solution lies in affirmation of 'the feminine, the caring part of humanity'.[4] Frank Opie, an authority on environmental education in South Africa, calls for education that will be holistic, balancing the left and right hemispheres of the brain – combining 'the western world-view of education that emphasises technological and scientific development' with 'artistic, creative growth'.[5] Geoffrey and Susan Jellicoe emphasise the aesthetic in their classic *The Landscape of Man*. They draw an analogy which links the romantic travellers who visited, described, taxonomised and painted this country in the eighteenth century, with South Africans of today:

71

*Just as in the Age of Enlightenment the growth of knowl-
edge was balanced in men's minds by a feeling for
romantic landscape, so in the modern world society is
turning to ecology not merely as an emotional relief but
because it knows instinctively that a lack of appreciation
threatens life itself.*[6]

Into this complex modern world have come, since 1982, a remarkable group of South African works of fiction for children and
young teenagers, which either deal specifically with conservation
issues or reflect upon people's relationship with the natural environment. We have already seen that the upsurge of translations of
animal folktales for children and the animal stories of Marguerite
Poland are to a certain extent part of this movement. The very fact
that the books are novels, short stories and folktales, and not non-
fiction, is itself remarkable, for until the 1980s the most significant
South African children's books on the subject of nature had been
autobiographical (most notably *Jock of the Bushveld* and *Bushveld
Adventures*).

That there should be an outpouring of children's fiction in the
1980s on environmental themes seems to vindicate Opie's call for
the involvement of the artistic, creative side of society. Fiction by
its nature deals with aesthetics, with ethical and moral issues, personal commitment, attitudes and conflicts of values – precisely
what Clacherty says environmental education should include. The
novels and stories do not have to be overtly didactic on the subject; indeed, that would nullify their affective potential. To what
extent the recent South African books also embody Ian Player's
feminine principle in their approach to environmental issues is examined in the course of my discussion.

Recent children's fiction on the environment: an overview

The following list of works under consideration in this chapter is
intended to facilitate reference.

- Elana Bregin, *Warrior of Wilderness* (1989)
- Vivienne Johns Brown, *The Boy and the Tree* (1989)

- Pieter W Grobbelaar, *The Earth must be Free* (1984)
- W.A. Hickey, *Manela the Bull Elephant* (1976)
- Dianne Hofmeyr, *When Whales go Free* (1988)
- Felicity Keats, *The Wild Swarm* (1987)
- Dale Kenmuir, *The Tusks and the Talisman* (1987)
  Song of the Surf (1988)
  Dry Bones Rattling (1990)
- Klaus Kühne, *The Secret of Big Toe Mountain* (1987)
- Mitzi Margoles and Sheila Hoffenberg, *Mandu and the Forest Guardian* (1987)
- Pieter Pieterse, *The Misty Mountain* (1985)
- Marguerite Poland, *Shadow of the Wild Hare* (1986)
- Patricia Prestyn-Thomas, *Moontide* (1987)
- Alix Prettejohn, *The Poacher of Hidden Valley* (1986)
- Peter Slingsby, *Leopard Boy* (1989)
- Hjalmar Thesen, *A Deadly Presence* (1982)
- Heinz Winckler, *In the Dead of Night* (1984)
- Peter Younghusband, *Kobie and the Military Road* (1987)

Of these nineteen, sixteen are English and the other three originally Afrikaans. The English books include all the significant works published after 1981 that can be classified as belonging to the theme. (Kenmuir has also written *Ol' Tangletooth,* but I have selected the three listed here as representative.)

The Afrikaans books in English translation have been included for comparative purposes, in order to put the English ones in a wider context. *Manela the Bull Elephant,* to which W.A. Hickey has written a companion story *Manela and the Poachers,* is one of many books by W.A. Hickey. It can be regarded as a transitional precursor of the environmental novels of the 1980s. *The Misty Mountain (Geheim van die Reënwoud)* is one of several by the author of Afrikaans youth novels, Pieter Pieterse, and *The Earth must be Free (Die Aarde moet Vry Wees)* is a picture book for young children by Pieter Grobbelaar, also a prolific children's writer.

It is, in fact, becoming difficult to distinguish in which language a children's book is originally written, since most are translated and published in both languages. The books do not give the names of the translators and there is often no indication that they are translations. In the case of *The Misty Mountain*, the English title does better justice to the contents than the original Afrikaans title does, since the latter, with its reference to a 'geheim' ('secret'), is inaccurate – a trite, sensational title for what is actually a gentle book. *The Wild Swarm* is an example of a book in which the translation, in this case into the Afrikaans *Die Wilde Swerm*, even changes the names of the characters, so that there is no hint for the Afrikaans reader of the perhaps less familiar ethos of the original. However, this sort of change is usually unnecessary, because in modern South African children's fiction English and Afrikaans-speaking characters are normally indistinguishable.

Most of the books are novels aimed at the young teenager, aged approximately eleven to thirteen. Three, *The Earth must be Free*, *The Boy and the Tree*, and *Mandu and the Forest Guardian*, are picture books for young children. *Warrior of Wilderness* is difficult to place, but might be read by nine or ten-year-olds if read at all. *A Deadly Presence* is usually listed as a youth novel, although it might have been intended for adults – its length and subject matter set it apart from the others. On the whole they make an impressive corpus of children's books, considering the novelty of the enterprise. The picture books are outstanding in design and illustration. The ideas for the plots of the novels are good, even if some of the writers are not too expert in the execution, which is where the absence of a strong tradition of children's fiction in South Africa shows up. Some memorable, highly individual characters have been created, and their environments and the issues in which they become involved are vividly evoked.

What is particularly intriguing is the prevailing mood of the novels – the typical personality of the central characters, their relationship with wild things, and the part that nature plays in exposing and developing their inner potential. Some of the books make the issue of environmental conservation part of the essence of the novel, creating the moral dilemmas, the tensions of the plots, and the conflicts within and between characters. A further level of complexity is to be found in those that create a metaphorical or even mystical connection between humans and nature.

The range of conservation topics covered suggests that this unprecedented rush of books with an environmental theme has been prompted by increasing awareness of ecological issues. To a large extent they are still concerned with the conservation of specific

74

species, though the range is greater than the 'flagship species' of the traditional game reserves. Now we have a variety of both fauna and flora, and the settings include the coast and sea, indicating a welcome extension of national consciousness from the traditional Bushveld heartland to include South Africa's vast marine possessions. The species that form the actual focus of the plots are otters, seals, whales, elephants, okapis, leopards, bushpigs, riverine rabbits, wild bees, wild birds, cycads, proteas and forest trees. A specific animal or plant obviously has more potential to generate a good plot than a broader ecological issue such as air pollution or environmental conservation. There are, however also some books dealing with broader ecological issues.

Much of the charm of the books lies in their evocation of their settings. In contrast to the overt presentation of scientific information in scientific language, descriptions of places, plants, animals and bird life are included incidentally, filling the books with enjoyable detail. A delightfully indigenous atmosphere is created by the unselfconscious use of colloquial terms. What helps to give these references such an authentic flavour is that in all but two of the books the protagonists actually live in the countryside where the action takes place; only in *Warrior of Wilderness* and *In the Dead of Night* are the children on holiday in an unfamiliar setting, and even in the latter the author refers to the natural setting in a taken-for-granted way. This marks a distinct move away from the Bushveld Syndrome concept of nature as a place of retreat from the city, and of white children as strangers in the land of their birth. While the children may still have things to learn about their environment, at least they have appropriated the topography. They are at home.

Fiction and science

Ironically, although these books are works of fiction, and although they take nature as their theme, they are much more modern and technological than the subject matter of English teaching was in the heyday of the Bushveld Syndrome. The child readers and the child characters are expected to take an interest in scientific information. Authors' notes give both historical and technical background information and acknowledge the assistance of experts such as scientists and game rangers. Dale Kenmuir goes further in introducing *Song of the Surf*: he not only says, 'I am indebted to fellow scientists and naturalists, whose diverse findings and observations, often won at hard cost, added to the substance of this tale,' but he goes on to apologise to them for the liberties he has taken by having a small seal island, Klein Ichaboe, blown up in the story, whereas in fact it still stands, unharmed. Marguerite Poland also includes a note apologising for moving the habitat of the riverine rabbit further east. It was, she says, artistically easier than moving the habitat of the child characters, which is an authentically depicted Eastern Cape farm.

Intriguing scientific names are used to good effect. One can imagine the reader savouring the strange words just as the child characters do. Poland reserves her information about the riverine rabbit, *Bunolagus monticularis*, for her note at the end, as it would not have been easy to bring it into the story, but the boys of *The Poacher of Hidden Valley* proudly pronounce the names of the cycads in order of rarity, *Altensteinii*, *Villosus* and *Caffer*; and the actual name of the protea, *Mimetes thunbergia*, thought to be extinct but rediscovered by the children in *The Secret of Big Toe Mountain*, is a key part of the mystery. We are also shown the children consulting the original work by Carl Thunberg in which he recorded his find.

Science is the actual theme of *The Wild Swarm*, but the story is a little too uncomfortably reminiscent of school to be altogether fun for young readers. After a Std 5 class are set a holiday science project by their teacher, a group of four discover the swarm and make a study of it. What they learn is told in detail, including an imposing list of reference works lent to them by a beekeeper whose advice they seek. The story is somewhat redeemed by the interaction of the four clearly delineated characters, and the development of the central character, Jeremy, from a shy, solitary boy who sleeps in his treehouse in the holidays, to a more selfconfident, sociable person. Incidental environmental information is provided by the beekeeper, who lives in Everton, Natal – a rather unusual setting for a South African children's book. He teaches local people 'of all races' how to collect wild honey and still protect the bees, and he runs a workshop for black women to weave basketwork hives. He is also the only example in the books of an health food exponent – he is mildly satirised when he lectures the children on the advantages of honey over refined sugar.

Even if not in the form of scientific facts, information about the ways of the wild is imparted by all the books. Some go further than others in describing 'nature, red in tooth and claw'. There are some graphic descriptions of mating and the birth of animals, as well as accounts of how mothers may overlie their young or devour them, and many other ways that death comes in the wild.

Adventure stories

At the simplest level some of the books are rather amateurishly written adventure stories. The earliest is Hickey's *Manela the Bull Elephant* (1976), redolent of an unsophisticated Bushveld era. The language of the English translation is inaccurate, unidiomatic, stilted and clichéd, and the plot is crudely constructed and unconvincing. It involves a youth who is protected by an elephant when he is lost in 'the Game Reserve', and who later returns as a probationer ranger and is able to save the elephant. In some of the worst parts of the book the author slips into an anthropomorphic mode in which human consciousness is attributed to the elephant, for example: 'He [Donald] glanced over his shoulder and saw Manela picking up marulas pretending not to see him walking away' (74).

That Hickey's books have an adult protagonist in itself sets them apart from the more recent books. Only two others, *The Tusks and the Talisman* and *A Deadly Presence*, also place an adult in this role. Of these, the latter is, as I have said, more of an adult novel, but *The Tusks and the Talisman* can be seen as parallel to *Manela* in that it is an early work, in this case the first novel by a writer whose subsequent works have child protagonists. (Kenmuir wrote *Dry Bones Rattling* and *Ol' Tangletooth* by popular request as what are sometimes called 'prequels', in which the boyhood adventures in the Kariba valley of the adult hero of *Tusks* are related.) *Tusks* belongs to an earlier tradition of boys' adventure stories which had adult heroes such as Biggles.

Although far superior to *Manela*, it is also a tough adventure story glorifying the work of game rangers. It creates a simple opposition: 'conservation and destruction' (36). The issues facing the dedicated conservationist, Tom Finnaughty of Kariba in Zimbabwe, are the preservation of game reserves, the pampering of wealthy foreign safari hunters who bring in the dollars needed for conservation, the combatting of poachers – in this case, a crooked ex-game ranger – unsympathetic bureaucracy, and inflexible, frustrating courts. The difference between this world and the pre-war struggles of Stevenson-Hamilton in the Transvaal lies in the new, mercenary aspects of keeping game sanctuaries viable:

> *A wilderness paradise lay beneath his gaze, where animals roamed in freedom as they had done for thousands of years. It was a remnant patch of wild country in a shrinking world. He knew that if the valley was to be preserved in a land-hungry country it had to pay for itself, and animals like M'tagati [a famous elephant] were the drawcards that helped the valley pay protection money to society. (71)*

Two aspects of the book show Kenmuir's talent as a writer. The beauty of his descriptive writing, in its detail and evocation of atmosphere, reflects his personal acquaintance with the country around Kariba. When the poacher is about to shoot the elephant,

> *A gentle breeze blew up the Zambezi, ruffling the cream tassle-tops of the river reeds. Cicadas shrilled monotonously in the surrounding trees, while up in the gorge a fish eagle called, the wild yodel echoing like some last-rite hymn for the doomed. (10)*

Secondly, his sympathy with nature increases his understanding of human nature. The Rhodesian Bush War and the poaching merge into one metaphor about the savagery of human beings:

> *In time the vile noises of man abated ... Nyamomba cottage was gutted and abandoned. The bush war left it a mere shell. No longer was there the throbbing of a generator or the clack-clack-clack of a water pump. No lights at night, nor the humming and whining of four-wheel-drive vehicles straining through the valley heat. No loud booming of hunting rifles, nor the smell of putrifying meat as trophy hides and skulls dried in the sun. No noisy whirlybirds settling down in a flurry of dust and leaves, nor the clatter of rifles and machine guns ... So the giant elephant moved out of the escarpment hills where he had lived for*

so long and took up residence at Nyamomba. He liked it there. He could bathe in the cool river, feed on lush reeds and sedges, climb the hills when the marulas were ripe, or wander through the valley in search of acacia pods and other delicacies. (7)

Sadly, the book degenerates into second-rate blood-and-thunder, exaggerated suspense, stock villains and ludicrous prose that does little justice to Kenmuir's lyrical descriptions of the bush:

Cronje stepped forward. 'In future, it's Mister Cronje to you, son. Understand?' He pushed the barrel of the pistol into Nesbit's nostril and lifted his head with a jerk ... A balled fist crashed into his mouth, snapping his head back and dropping him like a ripe marula. (124)

Both of the books that have the conservation of plants as their theme, *The Poacher of Hidden Valley* and *The Secret of Big Toe Mountain*, also fall into the category of flawed adventure stories. This is a pity because the authors had good ideas for their plots and both have a flair for conveying a sense of place and the flavour of the children's conversation.

The Poacher of Hidden Valley, by Alix Prettejohn, has an authentic-sounding setting on a farm and in a boarding school in the Eastern Cape. Farmers drive BMWs, the boys talk of 'Joeys' and make typical remarks such as ' "Sherbet," said Greg, "that's the closest I've ever been to being wiped out" ' (44). However, the plot becomes increasingly incredible as the two boys from neighbouring farms are blackmailed into stealing more and more cycads and snaring buck for an unscrupulous youth whom they met at school. Their escapades even lead to the starting of a veld fire and include springing someone from the local police cells. Prettejohn thinks he must multiply the action to increase the excitement. Equally incredible is the way the boys' misdeeds are, in retrospect, reduced in enormity and they are forgiven, except for their most serious offence, paying the little grandsons of a farm labourer to set snares for them.

Their adventures take place against a background of typical farm life in which hunting on a small scale is normal, and one can understand young Dale's question to his Dad as to whether they would be caught removing cycads on their own farm, which leads to the key lesson of the story:

> '*No, probably not,' said Mr Harris, 'but that's not the point. They are protected because they are becoming scarce, and it is up to each one of us to look after the ones we have.'*
>
> '*But surely, Dad, this is your farm and you can do what you like with it?'*
>
> '*Not really, son. I'm only "borrowing" this ground for my lifetime. I hold it in trust, for you and your children and future generations, the lives of all the creatures and plants that live here, and it is not for me to put their existence in jeopardy.' (50)*

Klaus Kühne's problem in writing *The Secret of Big Toe Mountain* is that he has far too much material to crowd into the very short 62 pages of the book. The story concerns Kim, a thirteen-year-old city girl, who reluctantly moves from Johannesburg to a village called Lancers on the edge of the Little Karoo when her parents buy a hotel there. Kühne deftly adds South African touches: Kim's hobby is to go horseriding at Halfway House, she enjoys eating pizzas at roadhouses, on the long drive to Lancers she listens to her walkman, and when they stop the car 'the air smelt of dust and orange peels' (7). The old hotel is perfectly described, particularly pleasing being the local word 'broekielace':

> *The low white structure had a steeply pitched, red corrugated-iron roof with a large, central gable. A grape vine straggled in and out of the intricate broekielace woodwork above the broad stoep…. Some of the stained-glass flowers in the front door lacked a petal or a leaf and the brass handle and bellpush hadn't been polished in ages. (12)*

In Lancers Kim meets a boy called Hennie Viljoen, with whom she discovers a few specimens of Thunberg's protea on a site which is earmarked for a spa hotel, and with the help of a conservation-minded journalist they stop the planned development. But squeezed in are a gymkhana, a mysterious light in a converted observatory on top of the mountain, and – in the space of four pages – a flood like the Laingsburg disaster which hits their village and destroys the hotel. The journalist, Mr Otto (who boasts, 'I stopped them building the saltworks at Rietvlei lagoon' [59]), articulates the environmental issues. He explains (though this is only in passing, which is the treatment everything receives) that the flood was partly due to overgrazing and the cutting down of trees; and he states the case for the protea and conservation:

We must stand up for the right of Mimetes thunbergia to survive unmolested. So much has been destroyed already that we must do our best to conserve what is left ... When we treat the small things of this world in a shabby way, we lose something of our humanity each time. (55)

The protea is saved, Kim is reconciled to living in Lancers and having a friend like Hennie, and Mr Otto delivers a South African *coup-de-grâce* to insensitive property developers: 'Neither he nor his sister nor anybody else will be able to build so much as a *kleinhuisie* up there with all the publicity the protea will be getting' (60).

A book in a class of its own is *Kobie and the Military Road* by Peter Younghusband. Unlike the other adventure stories with an environmental theme, it is extremely well written. However, although the plot concerns the efforts of little Kobie to stop a military road to the border being built through a vlei which a friend has turned into a bird sanctuary, and some detailed descriptions of the bird life, the interest of the book lies in Kobie's adventures and the people he meets. The Western Transvaal dorp and its people are affectionately and humorously portrayed, and Younghusband brings an authentic South African touch to the classic motif of the journey in children's books when he describes Kobie's journey to Cape Town to see the State President.

Younghusband's cynicism as a seasoned journalist is there for those who look: the road is protected by political trade-offs and corruption in high places, and the State President only cancels its construction because his wife persuades him that by doing so he will win the votes of women ('Aitsa!' exclaims the Minister of Internal Affairs admiringly at this stroke of political genius) – a sad commentary on the status of environmentalism in the Cabinet.

Picture books

Before we look at the other youth novels, there are the three children's picture books to consider. All three embody an attractive marriage of text and illustration, and are much more accomplished than most of the books we have looked at so far. The first two affirm the right of humans to exploit nature's resources, but teach that we must live in harmony with nature, while the third shows how humans are destroying nature. *Mandu and the Forest Guardian* concerns a Pygmy boy of the rain forest. He is the sort of little boy with whom the child reader (or listener) would love to identify, though the forest in which he is so happy is made to sound exotic to us. We are shown how his family band live in harmony with the forest when they arrive in a clearing to set up camp. The grandfather lights a fire from his fire stick and the band repeats after him an incantation, 'Thank you, our forest, for bringing us to this good place.' When Mandu gets lost, he befriends an okapi which leads him home. It is such a beautiful creature that Mandu believes it is a 'spirit guardian of our forest'. Next day it is driven in a game drive towards the hunters' nets, but Mandu pleads for its life, and the grandfather decrees that as okapis have become rare they will no longer be hunted.

Judging from the illustrations, *The Boy and the Tree* is about a black South African boy who lives in a simple Western-style house in the country. The language of the text suggests that the book is intended for speakers of English as second language: 'In the forest there was a fine tree, a tall tree – tall as ten men. The trunk did not curve or bend. Today he would cut it down. It would fall with a loud crash!' We are told all the uses to which the wood would be put. The creatures of the forest – green pigeon, duiker, mice, bush pig, chameleon – explain why they depend on the tree, and the owl is asked to adjudicate. The owl judges that since the tree is bound to fall one day, the boy should give it one year's grace, to give the creatures time to move, after which he may cut it down, on condition that he plants a sapling, which he does. 'The forest was filled with sunshine and song. The boy sang as he walked home. At last he had good wood to work with. The creatures sang because they were safe.' This conclusion reflects the rather pedantic tone of the text. Though attractive to look at, it is not as entertaining to read as the other two.

The text and illustrations of the Afrikaans book, *The Earth must be Free*, create comic effects of zaniness and quirky, peripheral oddities that should amuse the observant child. Although the illustrator, Alida Bothma, has also used collage in other books where the medium is simply distracting, it is a most appropriate medium here, for the story about littering is illustrated with pictures incorporating newsprint. In the story, the people of a village forget that the earth must be free, otherwise it dies, and they bury themselves in rubbish. At the last minute they are rescued with bulldozers, and a diaspora follows: they leave and change their names. But old habits die hard, for they continue to litter a little, and each day the earth dies a little.

The mysterious

The novels to which we come now are superior to the adventure stories that we have looked at so far. The interest of their plots is provided by the main theme of conservation without overcrowded action and melodrama, and by concentrating on the main theme the authors are able to explore its complexities with more subtlety. More complex, too, are the characters. Their involvement in the emotional and moral issues of conservation, their sense of the numinous in nature and the mystical bond between humans and nature, and the use by the authors of nature as an objective correlative for human experience, give the novels unity of plot and theme, and put the exploration of conservation on the holistic level that Frank Opie and Ian Player have called for.

Still rather at the level of the adventure story is *In the Dead of Night* by Heinz Winckler. Its title gives an exaggerated suggestion of mystery and adventure. The child characters, fifteen-year-old James Fraser and his thirteen-year-old sister Shirley, are if anything more colourless than the boys of Hidden Valley Farm (in *The Poacher of Hidden Valley*) and Kim and Hennie of Lancers (in *The Secret of Big Toe Mountain*). However, Winckler's plot is much more – though not entirely – credible, restricted to a series of events leading to the arrest of a poacher. While the children are on holiday at Hermanus they become interested in the clawless otters to be found there. From their observations they are able to give information to the local Conservation Officer that contributes to the capture of Logan, who poaches not only otters but also buck, baboons, genets, honey badgers and monkeys. The author tries to avoid over-simplifying good and bad by depicting Logan as a well-known character at the flea market where he sells his wares – he takes 'a craftsman's pride in the leather goods he made' (28), and we learn that he is saving up to become respectable. Scientific information about the otters is provided in the same way as in *The Wild Swarm*: the children consult an expert (the Conservation Officer) who refers them to reference books.

Through the people that the children meet the reader is shown many facets of conservation. Most important are the Conservation staff, who are depicted in a good light:

> *At the Nature Conservation offices a tall, affable young man in a khaki uniform with green epaulets received the Frasers. His uniform looked good on him and he had friendly blue eyes. (18)*

They also encounter conservation-minded farmers and an idealistic couple, the Macdonalds, who are starting up a small nature reserve:

> *'Mary and I feel that together we possess quite a bit of useful knowledge we should try to pass on to others, particularly the younger generation ... We would like one day to be able to offer a kind of ecological holiday course for children, from the southern countries of Africa for a start.' (79)*

On the negative side are a visiting English couple who unwittingly abet the poacher by purchasing his illicit venison and who later, after learning the truth, decide not to denounce him because they do not want to become involved. Winckler apparently included them to make a point, but their incorporation in the structure of the novel is ineptly handled and they fade out.

An aspect of the plot that is convincing is the growing interest of the Fraser family in the natural history of Hermanus, culminating in their commitment to the conservation cause. (Mr Fraser undertakes to find sponsorship for the Macdonalds.) Winckler clearly hopes that the reader will catch their enthusiasm: 'His wife Alice had identified several orange-breasted sunbirds, Cape sugar birds, tiny grey kapok birds, white eyes and a falcon' (16). The precise descriptions of the setting are enhanced by the use of popular names, as this example shows:

> *Every so often they would disappear in a shadowy tunnel*
> *of duine taaibos, Cape beech, milkwood and duine lepel-*
> *hout ... a rocky incline ... covered by a dense growth of*
> *coastal shrubs that reached over their heads ...fine leaved*
> *ironwood, Cape sumach, blinktaaibos. (3)*

In the Dead of Night is one of four of the novels (the others being *Shadow of the Wild Hare*, *A Deadly Presence* and *Leopard Boy*) that bring in a sense of dread about something mysterious, something inexplicable. It is the old fear of Darkest Africa felt by the earliest European visitors to the continent. At its most vulgar it is a conviction that beyond the surface realities of alien landscape, creatures and cultures must lie a world of voodoo. That the fears of fifteenth century Portuguese have remained part of popular white beliefs is evidenced by the long tradition of popular literature asserting that there is more to Africa than meets the eye: the novels of H. Rider Haggard; *Wide World* magazine; a stream of pseudo-scientific works purporting to give the true origins of Great Zimbabwe and Southern African rock art; the frequently reprinted books of Lawrence Green with titles such as *Great African Mysteries*, *Old Africa's Last Secrets*, *Strange Africa* and *There's a Secret Hid Away*; the books of Hedley Chilvers; T.V. Bulpin's yarns of lion-men and hyena cults in *The Hunter is Death*; Jan Juta's essays such as 'The secret' in *Look Out for the Ostriches*; Eric Rosenthal's *They Walk by Night*; N.G. Bezant's *Everlasting Footprints and Other Strange Stories of South African People*; Credo Vusamazulu Mutwa's *Indaba My Children* and *Africa is My Witness*; and Lyall Watson's *The Lightning Bird: the story of one man's journey into Africa's past*. The titles of the children's books, with their emotive words 'shadow', 'dead', 'deadly presence' and 'night', and mention of a weird 'leopard boy', hark back to these fears. However, *Leopard Boy* attempts to deconstruct the 'mystery' of Africa, as we shall see.

In three of the books female characters have an almost psychic awareness. James, in *In the Dead of Night*, pooh-poohs his sister's premonitions. Actually, one cannot blame him, for they are not portrayed very convincingly. Apparently Winckler is attempting to create suspense early in the novel, when Shirley is 'apprehensive' and James 'sensed his sister's uneasiness': ' "It's so strange and quiet here," she said, shuddering. "Let's go!" ' (5). Later,

> *Shirley stared at the forbidding pool under the bridge. Every now and then a lazy ripple moved across the opaque surface of the water almost as if, she thought, to cover up a dark secret. She shuddered.*
>
> *'There's something spooky about this place,' she whispered.*
>
> *'Don't be silly!' James scoffed. (29)*

Shirley's mysterious fears are not developed as the story progresses. If they are intended to suggest an intuitive suspicion of the poacher's nefarious deeds, then one can only say that the effect is one of bathos.

In *Shadow of the Wild Hare* Marguerite Poland has created a character, Rosie, who is far more complex than the child characters we have encountered in nature stories so far. Rosie is at the same time a rather bossy, practical farm girl and a sensitive, introspective young adolescent, whose fears and fantasies are therefore largely credible. Through her sensitivity the reader is made aware of the relationship between humans, animals and myth. In a world in which the well-being of human beings involves the death of animals (in this case, of the jackals that kill the goats), human beings nevertheless are part of creation and have ties with and obligations towards wild creatures and all defenceless things.

Poland rather overdoes the sense of dread at times – she is not always successful in managing the plots of her adolescent and adult novels – but other than that the story of Rosie's attempt to keep a wild hare is linked with legend in a subdued, convincing way. Her first encounter with the strange jackal-trapper is made to sound ominous:

> *The yard was very still. The only sound was the noisy sucking of the lamb. But suddenly something made Rosie turn, startled. It seemed as though even the cicadas had stopped their shouting to watch.*
>
> *There was a man standing by the kraal-wall. He carried a bag slung over his shoulder. He wore a coat*

*which hung about him like a loose, black hide. Rosie drew
in her breath, afraid he might have seen her squatting by
the pen. But he did not move. He stood quite still and
waited.*

*Rosie did not need to ask him who he was. She knew.
She had often heard her father talk of him. He was Tantyi
Mayekiso, the jackal-trapper. (4)*

When she calls her father to the yard, he senses something is the
matter, but 'she did not want him to know she was afraid'. Later
she goes with her father to the place where the trapper has his
camp, a place nobody normally visits because a diviner once died
there, and again Poland creates a foreboding atmosphere:

*It was very quiet. There was no wind to stir the grass. The
silence lay waiting among the sheds and outbuildings.
Here, no men went about their work in twos or threes, no
children trundled tyres down the road, guided with a stick.
Here, even the birds were different. They hid in the thorny
shade and watched with small dark eyes and fierce hooked
beaks to see who passed. There seemed to be no buntings
piping or dagbrekertjies calling in the new morning. Here
were jiza birds and jackie-hangers that flew up suddenly,
leaving hoppers dangling from a thorn. (17)*

Here Rosie finds the wild hare in the trapper's camp and, believing he will eat it, takes it home. Actually, he is using it as a bait
for jackals, but even that is mysterious, as she learns when a
neighbour, Tant Jacoba Pandoer, tells her, 'There was this old
Boesman. He told me it was used for *muti* to call jackals and *rooi-
katte*' (24). When Rosie realises that the hare is dying, she plucks
up courage to go back to the trapper. On this occasion, she re-
spectfully replaces a stone which has fallen from a fresh cut in a
boerboon tree:

*She knew it had been put there as an offering to the spirit
of the tree, just as travellers place stones on cairns and
say, 'Qamata, ndiphe amandla' – 'God, give strength to
me': a blessing for the journey. (36)*

We realise that Rosie sympathises with the traditional beliefs of the Xhosa people. Mayekiso explains that in captivity the hare has lost its *isithunzi* and will die, so she releases it when the phase of the moon is propitious.

The wild hare of the story is hardly a real creature; it is a creature of myth. Its elusive nature is typified by the uncertainty surrounding its name in the book. Because the riverine rabbit is so rare, hardly anyone has seen it, and it is known by various names, as well as being falsely identified. The uncertainty begins with the very title of the book, which Poland admits is wrong, although she defends it in her author's note:

> *I have called the riverine rabbit in my story Dhau, the hare, even though I am aware that 'riverine rabbit' is scientifically correct. I have done this because it is more likely that it would be referred to as a pondhaas, doekvoet or hare in the country districts, especially by farm children. Also in the San myth, it was a hare who asked the meaning of life and death from the moon. (86)*

Thus in the story it is called Hansie, Dhau, hare, *doekvoetjie*, *pondhaas*, and (mistakenly) a *kolhaas* (scrub hare). The slippery nature of names symbolises the elusive nature of all wild things, including the trapper himself. When he tells her the creature is called Dhau,

> *Rosie smiled to herself. 'Dhau,' she said softly, thinking of how they'd named him Hansie and how it would seem as strange to call him Hansie now as it would to think of Tantyi Mayekiso as Klaas or Jacob or Witbooi. (45)*

The legends told to Rosie about the riverine rabbit are also elusive, variously calling Dhau 'the child of the old people' and saying that he lives in the moon where his shadow grows as the moon waxes. Most significantly, Mayekiso tells her that as a wild creature the hare cannot live without its shadow, its *isithunzi*, which can only be restored by setting it free 'when the moon is small and Dhau can grow with it in brightness' (40). In a central passage, Rosie comes to understand what *isithunzi* means when she encounters a neighbouring farmer's pet baboon, Adoonsie:

She looked into his eyes. They were dark and empty. As

she gazed at him she knew, suddenly, that the small ba-
boon had lost his isithunzi. It was gone. Gone. He had lost
it when they'd tied a chain around his leg. Once he was a
wild thing. Now he sat on his perch begging fruit – eating
whatever people gave him. He might as well be dead.

She understood – at that moment, quite distinctly –
what isithunzi meant. It was light in the eyes, the taste of
the night, the freedom to hunt or to hide or to forage.
Isithunzi was being able to follow the little moon or to
watch the stars in quietness. How could there be isithunzi
without hope – with a pole and a chain or a hutch and a
bowl? (63)

The poignant aspect of the story is the revelation that Jacoba Pandoer, the slow-witted, squint-eyed woman, is the human equivalent
of the hare. Gradually we learn her story, of how she was taken as
a child from the farm labourers who cared for her after her grand-
parents died – the 'Boesmans' in their 'strooise', as her detractors
put it – and put in an institution in De Aar, from where she ran
away to the only people who loved her, but she was caught and
taken back. It is Jacoba who tells her, 'You will never make it
tame … It is a wild thing' (24), and poignantly, 'You should set it
free. Even if it dies. It is better than a cage. This thing I know'
(33). Rosie concludes,

Tantyi Mayekiso, it seemed to her, was all isithunzi – just
as though he were the ghost of the diviner that had lived
among the rocks where the kannabos grew up. And Jacoba
Pandoer? She had had one once even if she'd lost it like
Adoonsie. In the end, Rosie thought, it was better to have
lost it and be sad than never ever understand what
isithunzi was – never care or know what had been missed.
(65)

There is a unity of story, theme and symbolism in this novel that
elevates it to a profound level of understanding, not about 'conservation', but about the relationships between South Africa's
peoples, and between them and nature, yet at the same time it is a
book that is attractive and readable for young adolescents.

A sense of dread is central to *A Deadly Presence*, as the title implies. In this accomplished novel, by far the most sophisticated and exciting on our list, literal fears merge with metaphorical and metaphysical ones in the blackness of a man-eating leopard. The author, Hjalmar Thesen, is an established author who is a member of the well-known Thesen family of Knysna. He has taken a little licence to set his story about the leopard in the familiar country-side around Knysna, which he describes in superbly evocative language, stimulating the reader's visual, olfactory and auditory senses:

> *The peaty water was as black as tar where it was at all deep and yellow-gold or amber in the shallows, and yet in a glass it sparkled almost clear with neither mud nor sediment to cloud it but only those tasteless dyes from the ancient loam of the forest above. (4)*

> *The air too was still and warm and tinged with aromatic oils that the sun had drawn out of the forest: a kind of vaporous honey, compounded of both herb and flower. (3)*

> *The time passed winging high as the cormorants overhead, tumbling on the cries of oyster catchers, running with the endless eddying and chuckle of the sea. (105)*

This perfect, golden setting is invaded by the leopard, driven initially to eating human flesh by an injury caused through a bungled attempt to shoot him with a gun-trap, but subsequently becoming addicted to his abnormal taste. His blackness is a freak of nature and comes to symbolise for different people their darkest fears.

Cliff Turner, a young scientist doing research on leopards, despises white people who through complacence and ignorance fear Africa:

> *The mountains looming blue in the background and the forest beneath were nothing more than a scenic backdrop to the beach life and the tinkling of ice in glasses and the swaying of dancers. The gregariousness of human occupation and its pursuit of comfort did not permit much interest in the land or the life of the land, especially if it were in any way uncomfortable: and the forest was uncomfortable;*

so were the mountains except as scenery and so basically
were the poorer whites on their smallholdings and the even
poorer Coloured people. (7)

Not surprisingly, when the black leopard starts his rampage, the
local people react with hysteria, and the press with sensationalism.
Cliff develops his speculations about white people's fears of black
when he quotes Van Wyk Louw's poem, 'Die swart luiperd'. He
argues that the poem is an attempt by an Afrikaner to establish
black as pure so that 'a beautiful black woman could be desired
naturally without the Calvinistic conscience'; upon which he is
warned that he is 'an outsider prying into the mystical heart of
Afrikanerdom' (74).

The black leopard takes on a different significance for the
young widow, Joan Mannion, on whose farm it often prowls: 'Perhaps even in her subconscious there stirred too an ancient
remembering of the dangers of darkness soon to come: an atavistic
instinct not quite dormant' (7). The leopard becomes for her an
avatar of human beings' ancient enemies:

It was as though some long-dormant sense had awakened
in her, opening a door in her brain to reveal the ghosts of
terrors from a vanished time: the frozen winds of an Ice
Age, the snuffling of a cave bear at the bouldered en-
trance, the very breath of some great feline hunter; ... she
knew with absolute certainty that she was a prey animal,
cornered and alone and linked through time to those others
whose bones had been dust for a hundred thousand years.
(138)

The thought of the leopard haunts her nights, evoking archetypal
fantasies of anthropomorphism and lycanthropy. Although the
author does not make it explicit, but is hinted at by Cliff's interpretation of the poem, the leopard becomes a sexual symbol for
Jean: this time not the desired black female, but the black male
that prowls around her house at night and eventually, in a moment
of horror, breaks into her bedroom.

Atavistic fears are not, however, the only concern of the novel.
Through the character of Cliff Turner, Thesen takes an unusual
look at some of the political and moral aspects of conservation in

South Africa. Cliff is an affluent English-speaking liberal who acknowledges that he is one of a group 'whose forefathers had engineered much of the wealth of the country and who once had lorded it over all their fellow-countrymen, including the Afrikaans-speaking whites' (21). He identifies economic and political privilege with 'the place and responsibility of mankind as an animal species in the limited habitat of the earth's surface' (20). But he realises that it was capitalism that 'developed' the country, leading to the destruction of the leopard's natural habitat and its prey; it is capitalism, 'the protection of wealth' (121) (in the form of the landowner, Jean, and the lavish research grant that Cliff enjoys), that artificially tries to preserve the leopard against the interests of white farmers and local black people.

Like his forefathers, Cliff interferes with the balance between humans and nature, but he does it by trying to protect the leopard, only to see it cause further harm. He knows that he is quixotic. When Polly, an Afrikaans conservation officer's wife, asks him, 'Why are you so crazy about leopards in any case? What good do they do?' he replies, 'Destruction, Polly, I'm in favour of life, that's all. There's enough prejudice in this country already,' to which she retorts, 'You rooinekke! You're funny people' (27).

The leopard crystallises the moral condition of the English-speaking liberal. Early in the book Cliff admits that he is 'a member of a lost group, suspect, powerless: one of the minority of a white minority, the now impotent English-speakers' (21). Later he analyses the reasons for the once-powerful English having reached this state:

> *It's not all that easy to be free. The whole ethos of English freedom of thought is all very well and natural in the UK itself and in Europe, but in present-day Africa it's a different proposition. It's – it's like a positive charge in an atmosphere made negative by prejudice, skin colours, languages, cultures, and I'm not only thinking of black and white difference. It's seeing all points of view and understanding the motivations and in the process becoming impotent, sort of negatively stuck. (74)*

Almost as an act of reparation to those who have suffered, Cliff risks his life as a human bait for the leopard. The strategy is successful, and the leopard is captured for a zoo.

A Deadly Presence is the only one of our conservation novels that entertains the theory that conservation of glamorous mammals – the 'flagship species' – is an elite enterprise which may become an abuse of power. As an interpretation of the colonial history of South Africa, this is not so far-fetched, as John M. Mackenzie has shown in *The Empire of Nature: Hunting, Conservation and British Imperialism*, where he argues that the colonial elite inherited the medieval European tradition that hunting was a pastime for the privileged elite, who labelled subsistence hunting as 'poaching' and proscribed it; and that the first impetus for the conservation of wild animals came from the hunting lobby, who took possession of the animal life as the colonists had of the land.[7] In bringing together in one novel reflections upon ownership and the use of wealth, and atavistic fears of the black unknown, Thesen has written a book that goes deep into the white South African psyche, as can be seen by comparing it with a passage from Van Wyk Smith's *Grounds of Contest* in which he discusses the theme of miscegenation in South African literature:

> *In a colonial discourse of domination in which land, indigene and woman are so often transformations of one another, the white man's possession of the black woman has further obvious implications. In this context miscegenation confirms not only the white colonist's control over the possessed feminine 'terrain' and his access to the inner, hidden life of his subject, but, conversely, also his primal horror of being thus possessed by the alien mystery.[8]*

Leopard Boy, by Peter Slingsby, is the fourth novel linking nature with the mysterious unknown. It explicitly explores the legend of a therianthropic creature that is half-human, half-leopard – either literally, or else in effect: the feral child that has taken on the attributes of a wild animal. The creature becomes the object of people's fears of the unknown, though in this case without the sexual overtones of the black leopard in *A Deadly Presence*. Slingsby purports to demystify the story of the leopard boy of Waaihoek by referring in his author's note to the actual disappearance of a boy called Ebraime in the area in 1965, and the occurrence of the earthquake in the Boland in 1969, but this does not finally lay the ghost, for as he acknowledges, 'It is a timeless story, a legend told many times before, with many times yet to be told. Is there any truth in it, or is it merely another universal legend?' (121)

Furthermore, the novel is not a satisfactorily rational explanation of the legend, for that part of the plot which explains how the boy came to take on the skin cloak and ways of a leopard is not very convincing, and the story deliberately ends inconclusively, not revealing whether the boy still lives.

For all that, the story marks a change from the first great children's classic on the theme of the feral child, Kipling's Mowgli stories (in *The Jungle Books*), written a century ago. Those stories, written at a time of supreme imperialist confidence, are a fantasy, which explore what it would be like if we could, while remaining human beings with all the superior gifts of a higher order, talk with animals and learn their lore. Although Mowgli rejects what is unseemly in humans – after a period of return to their life as a youth he goes back to the animals – nevertheless in the end he rejoins human society and ends up with a government pension. By contrast, *Leopard Boy* comes after a century of disillusionment about the superiority of humans, and there can be no return to their world for the Leopard Boy.

Ebraime, the Leopard Boy, is the product of social deprivation, a street child from Cape Town who, like Jacoba Pandoer of *Shadow of the Wild Hare*, is put in a children's home. After being sent to work on a farm, he is attacked by a leopard which partly dehumanises him. Unlike handsome, articulate Mowgli, he loses his human features and his voice, although he does retain his intelligence. He is driven into the wilderness by people's unreasoning, superstitious fears. The book emphasises that people, not nature, are at fault. Those who are closest to nature – Wynand, a solitary farmer's son who collects insects, and a couple of mountain hikers – are not afraid of him.

> *'People scare me,' he [Wynand] said. 'I like it here on the mountain – there are no people.' He groped for the right words. Sitting there next to that extraordinary figure, the missing boy draped in a skin, it seemed more important than anything else that he should find the right words.*

'People ... other people always want you to do things ... to be things that you don't really want to be.' (60)

The hikers' commitment is not as complete as Wynand's. To Ebraime, they have a flaw: 'The great bowl of mountains seemed to call him – to say, come and explore, come and stay here. He wondered why the climbers came here. Did they also feel that strange call, to explore and stay? Why did they always leave and go home then?' (42). Although they believe in him and leave him food, Harry, one of the couple who befriend him, ultimately misunderstands and wants to reduce him to the fate that Kipling found inescapable and inevitable for Mowgli – Harry will obtain training and a job for him. But at the end of the twentieth century such a fate is no longer unambiguously desirable. Wynand articulates Ebraime's response: 'People don't want other people to be free. They want them to be like themselves – to keep them close where they always know whose they are and what they're doing' (104). His is the same cry from the heart as that of poor Jacoba Pandoer: it is wrong to cage the human spirit.

Whereas Mowgli haughtily lords it over the animals, Ebraime stops killing wild creatures, befriends a baby baboon, and even frees a leopard from a trap in spite of having been mutilated by one. The descriptions of his natural environment and the harmony between the two boys and nature convey to the young reader a message of the beauty of nature and the desirability of understanding and loving it. Slingsby, who has written several children's books set in the Cape, is himself a prominent conservationist and founder of ECCO, the Ecological Club for Children. He describes both the wide sweep of the landscape and the details of its wildlife:

> *[Ebraime] learned the haunts and habits of the buck, the small cats, the dassies, the mongoose ... He plunged into the great basin that lay behind the Waaihoek peaks and discovered the magic of the Witels River Gorge – the deep, dark pools which tunnelled through the mountain, the majestic waterfalls, the sweet, soft, crystal water that took his breath away because it was so cold. [He shows Wynand.] Wynand in return taught him about the insects of the mountain. He showed him the ant-lions, the robber beetles,*

*the curious butterfly larvae that lived in the nests of the
ants, licked and caressed by the ants themselves while they
murderously ate the ants' own young. (64)*

Eventually, the Leopard Boy is so close to nature that, like the
animals, he can sense the impending earthquake, and makes his
escape. Wynand, and the reader, need not grieve, for we know that
Ebraime is happy.

The feminine principle

At the beginning of this chapter I quoted Ian Player as saying that
ecological survival required the awakening of 'the feminine, the
caring part of humanity'. In some of the books that I have already
discussed this principle has been seen to provide the psychic en-
ergy: Jeremy, the quiet catalyst for the children's enthusiasm for
studying the wild swarm; the sensitivity of Rosie; the other-
worldliness of the Leopard Boy and the withdrawn personality of
his friend Wynand. Admittedly, those books that give female characters a sixth-sense – *In the Dead of Night*, *Shadow of the Wild
Hare* and *A Deadly Presence* – reinforce sexist stereotypes to
varying degrees: James mocking his sister's fears; Rosie surrounded by scoffing boys who like shooting; Jean, the helpless
female, depending on Cliff for protection. What is remarkable
however, is that so many of the central characters in all the conservation novels are in fact male, but do not fall within a typically
male stereotype.

According to a contemporary South African critic, Hilda
Grobler, if one were to postulate a null hypothesis for modern
boys' books, it would be that they stereotype boys as prime examples of machismo:

*The heroes in boys' books are extraordinary people and
they always have all the qualities a masculine male should
have, e.g. extremely specialised skills and/or a high degree
of technical competence in his particular field; great physical endurance; sharp and agile minds; numerous brain-
waves; unparalleled courage; resourcefulness; a vast
knowledge of all sorts of things such as explosives, the
technicalities of motor cars and motor bikes; great physi-*

cal strength; determination; fearlessness.[9]

Grobler does not quote any evidence for this generalisation, but it does provide a reminder of what the boy protagonists of our stories are *not*. Even the three adult male heroes, we are assured by their authors, are not overly masculine. The hero of *Manela, the Bull Elephant* is 'soft-spoken' (55), Tom of *The Tusks and the Talisman* is set apart from the other, swashbuckling, men by his sensitivity, integrity and idealism, and Cliff of *A Deadly Presence* has 'a vulnerable mind' (120).

The children's books we are discussing here fall within one particular tradition of English children's literature, which Peter Hunt has called the 'naturalist-mystic'.[10] In the late nineteenth century, when children's books written for entertainment became a recognisable genre, the most common were adventure stories such as those by Captain Marryat, G.A. Henty and R.M. Ballantyne. *Tom Brown's Schooldays* (1857) gave rise to the enormously popular school stories which propagated Victorian masculine values. Later, boys' books with all-conquering adult heroes such as detectives and the armed services characters of Percy F. Westerman followed. But in 1877 a completely different kind of book appeared which was seminal in creating the minority 'naturalist-mystic' tradition: *Bevis*, by Richard Jefferies, depicted a boy spending an idyllic summer holiday on his own and with a friend, absorbed in his own world in the countryside and splashing around on a lake. It was an early hint of the 'back-to-nature' movement that swept Europe in the early twentieth century, culminating in the success of the Boy Scout movement. In similar vein, Kenneth Grahame, author of *The Wind in the Willows*, wrote *The Golden Age* (1895) which, though not usually regarded as a children's book, described a group of children spending their happy days away from bothersome adults. After these two forerunners, the naturalist-mystic tradition was firmly launched in the twentieth century by Frances Hodgson Burnett's influential children's novel, *The Secret Garden* (1911). Not only did it lead to classics like the Arthur Ransome stories, in which children create a partly make-believe world in which adults leave them free to play in the outdoors, but with its theme of solitary children it was also suited to the growing popularity of children's literature portraying the psychological development of adolescents, of which the great example is *Tom's Midnight Garden* (1958) by Philippa Pearce.

The books we are concerned with are firmly in this tradition. Some of them, as we have seen, still have traces of the Enid Blyton 'Famous Five' tradition that children on their own can have real-life adventures catching crooks, but they have more realistic concerns. Their authors have rejected the male stereotypes of the Bushveld Syndrome, which can be defined in Lanham's terms as 'masculine and physical toughness, gregariousness, in-group cohesion and conformity',[11] and which perpetuated the image of colonialism as masculine rape of the country. Instead, the protagonists are usually solitary, introverted boys who, by the everyday norms of their circle, are unpractical, emotionally weak, fey. They possess a rapport with nature, an attitude towards it that is propitiatory, like Rosie's, and even sacrificial.

The shift from the Bushveld Syndrome is typified by the difference between the two Afrikaans books, *Manela, the Bull Elephant* and *The Misty Mountain*, which both tell the story of a boy growing up to become a game ranger. The difference begins with the titles: from the masculine world of the Eastern Transvaal Lowveld with its bull elephants we move to the soft, misty world of the Eastern Transvaal escarpment. *The Misty Mountain* describes a solitary, sensitive boy growing up in the forest, tenderly caring for his grandfather and his pet wild animals. The harshness of nature, the inevitability of death, and the facts of human exploitation of animals and forests are matter-of-factly handled, but the atmosphere is predominantly idyllic, gentle and cosy, sometimes overly romantic. The natural world of the forest is lovingly recreated for the reader, filled with bird calls, trees and shrubs each with its unique character, and wild creatures, of which the wild pigs are the most important in the story. As the boy Zachariah grows up, his sensitivity is tempered with lessons about cruel reality, culminating in the moment when he realises that the wild boar that will have to be shot is the one he once kept as a pet piglet, and he retches at the thought.

The theme of the novel, that people should live in harmony with nature, is conveyed in three ways. One of these is the extensive use of the pathetic fallacy, by which nature is made to reflect the actions and emotions of the human characters, such as when the drought is broken by a storm when Zachariah declares his love for his childhood sweetheart. The second is a charming conceit about birdcalls which the grandfather entertains, that 'They say exactly what you want them to say. You just have to listen' (126). Thirdly, because of his close acquaintance with nature, the grandfather makes nature an objective correlative for human behaviour. When he warns young Zachariah that it is not wise to keep wild creatures as pets because they 'always go away later' (40), he is thinking of his own experience of the loss of the boy's mother and the inevitable departure of the boy one day.

The two novels dealing with the conservation of marine wild life – *Song of the Surf* and *When Whales go Free* – contain the moodiest, most introspective boys. Dale Kenmuir had come a long way from *The Tusks and the Talisman* when he wrote *Song of the Surf*, a story about a lonely child living on the coast of Namibia. The unlikely setting of Namibia had already produced a precedent for the withdrawn waif, when Freda Linde published in Britain in 1975 her own English translation of an Afrikaans children's book that she had published two years earlier, entitled *The Singing Grass*. In this fine novel she tells the story of a shy boy who stutters so severely that he can only relate to his books and the pathetic, dying camel that he is employed by a farmer to mind. A couple who are setting up a game reserve offer him a job and, through his feeling for animals, they draw him out, setting him on the road to becoming a game ranger. Now, in *Song of the Surf*, we find a little boy, eleven-year-old David, and Mary, a marine biologist, ranged against David's father and other men determined to kill the seals that they believe are destroying the fishing and guano industries. In both books the severe men bred by the harshness of Namibia are impatient of intellectualism and feelings. Malgas Meintjies, headman of the fishing company, confronts Mary with 'You're for the seals, aren't you? I might have known. All women are soft on cuddly little seals' (44).

David, in the eyes of Mary, is a tiny though courageous opponent of the might of the fishing industry and government officials:

Who was this appealing little boy, with honest brown eyes, she wondered, living like some youthful Robinson Crusoe on this wind-swept island? ... The boy lifted his leg onto the bench and was picking scabs off his wound, his face concealed by an upraised knee. How often did he bath? Dirt and grime lined his ears, and his fingernails were

---

filthy. A neglected urchin, she thought. (18, 20)

In David's eyes, his father's rejection of him after his mother's death – 'He'd had love and sympathy before, but it had dried up' (12) – is compounded by his father's role as leader of the fishermen's lobby to have the seals killed, and David's reaction is to burst out, 'He's a bastard, and I hate him!' (59).

Human love and love of animals are intertwined in an ingenious plot that combines a psychological study of David with an informative and by no means one-sided account of seal culling. Mary, whose husband and baby were killed in a car accident, longs to give love to David, who has turned to animals and birds to fill the emotional void in his life. David's father, in his grief, has been unable to communicate with the boy. Rather less convincingly, the novel hints at an awakening romantic interest between Mary and the father. The author exploits these tensions to create an exciting narrative with some splendid moments, such as the denouement when David reveals to Mary that he is the son of the man who wants the seals killed: 'He's my father, miss. My surname is Woltemaarde. I am David Woltemaarde' (25). Another high point is when David writes a note to his father, saying he loves him, just before David expects to die with the seals when their island is dynamited (though he decides to escape just in time).

The lesson of the novel is that a solitary bond with animals is not enough; people need other human beings. In this way *Song of the Surf* reminds us of other nature novels. *Leopard Boy* for example shows that sometimes it is too late to make the connection with other people, and the ability to socialise, to be a true human, slips from one's grasp, or it is destroyed by other people as it was for Jacoba Pandoer.

Kenmuir identifies four different factors at work in the issue of seal culling: economics (Mary thinks of the fishermen 'always treading the thin line between sound conservation and damaging exploitation' [64]), scientific information, political expediency and sentiment. In this case, enough information is given to show that the threat of seals to the fishing industry is at best unproven, and since there is no talk of 'harvesting the natural resource' of seals, but simply a plan to blow them up, feelings in the end are vindicated even though the islet is destroyed.

The climax is rather too melodramatic. Unfortunately, Kenmuir still commits egregious lapses of style and good taste (such as the pretentious single-sentence opening paragraph, 'In the beginning there was a birth' [1]). There is enough intrinsic interest in the characterisation and the theme, without resorting to sensationalism.

When Whales go Free by Dianne Hofmeyr treats a subject that is just as topical and prone to sentimentality as the protection of seals. She tells the story of the fictional family of the historical figure, Odland, who established the whaling station on Beacon Island at Plettenberg Bay, from their arrival in 1912 until it closed down in 1916. Once again the tension is between the oppositional forces of the masculine killers and the feminine qualities of wildness and pre-industrial harmony between human beings and nature. This was Dianne Hofmeyr's second youth novel, and it confirms that she is one of South Africa's best children's writers. She tells an enthralling story with a strong, sympathetic child protagonist, set in a beautifully evoked milieu.

Whaling is shown to have been a legitimate business which the Odland family had practised with skill and pride for generations. By 1912, however, its integrity was beginning to be questioned: the Norwegian government had banned whaling (which made the opportunity to open the Cape station a godsend) and modern technology had stripped whaling of its heroic mystique, as the grandfather admits: 'It was a real contest. Man against beast! Each fighting for his life. No engines, steel boats and explosive harpoon guns on the side of man' (65).

The scion of the family, fourteen-year-old Eric, has always looked forward to the day when he can become a harpoonist, but before he is permitted to go on his first hunt he begins to encounter different values. He learns the effects of industrialisation: 'The face of the island was completely different now. And somehow, despite the excitement of the new station, he missed the emptiness and cleanness of the sandy hump' (10). Harking back to the idyllic life of the original inhabitants of Robberg, the Reverend Mr Sharples tells him:

There was plenty of buck and an abundance of shellfish – mussels, oysters, limpets – as well as grasses and birds' eggs to eat. And the caves and overhanging slabs of rock provided shelter from rain and wind. It was a perfect place to live ... The people had animal skins for clothing, karos-

ses and grass to make their beds comfortable, stone to make sharp tools from and seashells to make jewellery and ornaments. (48)

Although Eric does not admit it, the reader can tell from the description of the butchering of the whales and frequent reference to the pervading odour that the gory facts of whaling are not easy to become inured to. Finally, the morality of whaling is explicitly questioned by a girl called Aletta, who is a wild, dreamy creature of the forests, very like her counterpart, Nina, of Dalene Matthee's *Fiela's Child*. When Eric asks her why she released a bluebuck from her father's trap, thus risking a boating, she replies, 'Bluebuck must go free,' and asks him, 'Who will let the whales go free?' (50).

This novel lends itself to a classic structuralist analysis. Structural anthropologists – most notably, Claude Levi-Strauss and Edmund Leach – propound a theory of binary oppositions, showing that the boundary between antinomies is a potent source of ambivalence. Where the oppositions meet, simple categories overlap and blur, becoming a 'source of anxiety'.[12] Eric Odland finds himself in this conflicting position. The moment of anagnorisis comes when he goes on a whale hunt. He discovers to his horror that it is customary to kill a baby whale first in order to ensure that the adults will stay in the vicinity. When the whale is shot, the author uses the technique of the pathetic fallacy to convey Eric's oneness with nature in a scene reminiscent of those that portray the sensitivity of Zachariah in *The Misty Mountain*:

A fringe of rain was creeping up over the sea. It had already blocked out the horizon. A strange emptiness took hold of him. It was as if there was a great hollow somewhere in his chest, a longing ... He clung to the rail in the drenching rain and vomited over the side. (73)

Eric's loyalty to his family and his manliness are in question, not least through the continual snide remarks of his termagant sister. But by refusing to become a whaler he is liberated in the way that Edmund Leach has shown is characteristic of the twilight zone between oppositional propositions: 'Spatial and temporal markers which actually serve as boundaries are themselves abnormal, timeless, ambiguous, at the edge, sacred.'[13] He runs away to the solitude of Robberg where, although he cannot physically hear the song of the whales, he is acutely aware of their existence and the world they inhabit, and we know that in a sense their calls, which he has always strained to hear, have reached him. The sub-plot also reveals that he has always been 'abnormal, ... at the edge' because he established a sincere friendship with Aletta and her brother long before it is cruelly pointed out to him that he should have nothing to do with them because they are 'coloured'.

When Whales go Free ends on an optimistic note with Eric deciding to stay in South Africa when his family returns to Norway. However, the conclusion of the book shirks a couple of issues. The timely decision to close the station removes the necessity of deciding what should be done about Eric's refusal to work for his father. The historical reasons for the closure of the station, which Hofmeyr enumerates in her author's note, to some extent nullify the message of the book, for the whales go free for economic reasons, not because environmentalists won.

Fantasy

If one is going to explore conservation through fiction rather than science, then fantasy may be regarded as the ultimately different form that the fiction can take. Fantasy meets the plea of Frank Opie that the 'reductionist, building-block model of reality', the 'partial view' of 'classical science', should be replaced by 'a holistic, dynamic model which recognises interconnected relationships', one that will 'reach the whole child – physical, mental and spiritual being'.[14] Two fantasies stress this unity. *Moontide* by Patricia Prestyn-Thomas pleads for a time when humans will realise the interdependence of all living creatures and nature. She has a dolphin say, 'It's as though we belong together. Each part of the whole. And, somehow, sometime, we *shall* unite' (100). *Warrior of Wilderness* by Elana Bregin is a book in which the whole being of a boy is involved in a battle to save the integrity of nature.

These are two of four modern South African children's fantasies on the theme of a titanic battle with the forces of darkness, the others being *The Battle of the Mountain* by Judy Chalmers and *Witch Woman on the Hogsback* by Carolyn Parker. In the latter two matters of conservation are implicitly involved, but the emphasis is on the evil force. The books are visionary in depicting both black and white humans, animals and mythical beings uniting in fighting the threat to the survival of the world. The Witch Woman of the Hogsback seeks control of the Xhosas' mythical People of the River and People of the Sea, which would give her control of the waters, and she is also a threat to animals and birds, whom she enslaves along with humans, tokoloshes and mythical creatures. The heroine of *The Battle of the Mountain*, young Pippa, is chosen to fight the monster Igwain because of her special power with animals. When she confronts Igwain, she draws upon her special identification with nature, which she has felt all her life:

> *Mustering all her strength she sent a retaliatory beam of her own, a beam made up of thoughts of love for her fellow creatures, of her desire to use her gifts to help those she could, of wanting to share the good things of her land with all creatures. (129)*

Fantastic battles against Evil, especially involving a quest, subterranean tunnels, chthonic spirits and noble anthropomorphic animals, which are features of all four of these books, are themes as old as human storytelling, but unfortunately since the publication of the modern classics by C.S. Lewis, J.R.R. Tolkien, Alan Garner and Ursula Le Guin, new works employing these elements give the impression of being derivative. (The heroine of *Witch Woman on the Hogsback*, thirteen-year-old Kate, actually calls her search for the witch a 'quest', an improbably articulate and self-conscious labelling.) In the case of both *Moontide* and *Warrrior of Wilderness* this apparent derivation combines with the sheer ineptness of the writing to produce disappointing books.

Moontide is not a particularly *South African* book. The author was born in Britain but lives in Johannesburg, and the book was published in England. It is set in the oceans, and has a more universal than particular setting and plot. Its rather confused plot concerns the opposition of dolphins, whales and mantas to a conspiracy by the Orcas (killer whales) to take over the world by destroying humans. The Orcas temporarily win over most of the sea mammals with the argument that humans are destructive, and this gives the author the opportunity to recount gruesome details of the destruction of marine life through the dumping of toxic waste and other rubbish, pollution, whaling, and indiscriminate fishing, including the use of gill nets. The author even introduces a dolphin who has been reduced to a Zombi-like state by his time spent performing in a dolphinarium. The dolphins are shown to be loving, caring creatures, in some ways superior to human beings, and much interesting information about marine mammals is incidentally included. The dolphins' nobility is stressed by making them the heirs to Poseidon, with a high priest who controls the power to change the phases of the moon, resulting in the inundation of the earth. A core of the creatures believe, however, that 'the terrestrials have never been closer to enlightenment' (30). They have an ancient prophecy:

> *Many of the scourges presently endured by the humans would be eliminated. With our guidance and co-operation they could learn to farm the seas and harvest its* [sic] *bounty so that neither plants nor fish were depleted, and the vital balance sustained* [sic]. *(47)*

The story ends optimistically with the young hero, Boi, who defeats the Orcas and saves the high priest's heir, thinking:

> *And the terrestrials? What of them? Would they be ignorant of their place in nature's scheme much longer? Boi thought not. He had high hopes for the terrestrials. WONDERFUL, MARVELLOUS, HOPES* [sic]. *But for now, he must rest. (138)*

This is followed by a note listing some developments in the Greens movement and the banning of whaling.

The quotations above will have indicated the poor quality of the writing. The diction is riddled with clichés and vacillates between 'high', pseudo-archaic English thought suitable for noble creatures, science fiction utterances such as 'I tuned into my sensory lobe and am now in full-ocean-audial' (19), and bluff, 'lower class' language such as speaking of 'young 'uns'. The author also has difficulty with her grammar, particularly pronouns: 'The life blood of he whom I loved,' (91) and 'One whom, in trying to expose Tonaz's treachery, was himself unjustly banished' (131).

Warrior of Wilderness is also badly written. Much of the storytelling is childish (such as the creation of the stereotyped, selfish fat boy called Cedrick), yet the writing seems addressed to an older readership, with sentences such as ' "Oh, bugger Cedrick!" he muttered crossly' (6) and 'The repetition gave a neutral focus to his overwrought mind' (92). The quest for the 'Life Flame' that the hero, Danny, sets out on is predictable, but why he is chosen for this task is never really explained.

As a conservation tract the book propagates a message which might at first appear appealing but is actually bankrupt. First, human beings are blamed for having slaughtered what are, in fact, the 'flagship species', and then it emerges that what is wanted is a return to a pristine paradise such as existed before humans appeared on earth. So it is not, after all, a call for a balanced ecosystem in which humans have a place and a responsibility.

In spite of these weaknesses, any emotional identification that the reader might invest in Danny can have a powerful effect. Danny is another boy who, perhaps because of his 'feminine' qualities, has rapport with nature: 'He would have given anything to be tough and loud-voiced and bold; but he wasn't. He was just himself; and there was nothing he could do about it' (4). His quest is the classic Jungian journey of spiritual searching, an inward battle between good and evil leading to maturity. When he finally confronts the protean Evil One, it appears as his double and he must face up to his own complicity as a human being in the evil that is destroying the world. (This idea of the Evil One's taking on the hero's shape at the moment of truth has already been used by Ursula Le Guin in the *Earthsea* series.) And the identification goes further: Danny has to become the Redeemer who takes upon himself the sins of the world and saves the Life Flame through shedding his sacrificial tears. He has been told, 'You must have faith in yourself ... Whoever seeks [the Sacred Fire] must travel a hard, lonely route there; and travel it alone' (85). No-one can deny that humankind is in need of someone like Danny to expiate its guilt:

[He wept] for all darkened Wildernesses, the lost Edens that the Dark Devourer had destroyed, for all the wild, free, glorious things the earth once knew, but never would again. (134)

It is a pity that even at this climax the book should echo another classic, in this case the conclusion of William Golding's *Lord of the Flies*, when 'Ralph wept for the end of innocence, the darkness of man's heart, and the fall through the air of the true, wise friend called Piggy' (248).

Danny learns that in finding your true self you save Wilderness, and in saving Wilderness you fulfil yourself. This might also be said to be the experience of all the leading characters in the books discussed in this chapter.

Commitment and silence

The rough categories in which I have placed the books discussed in this chapter indicate what the mainspring of their action is. The child protagonists engage with something which creates the dramatic tension of the novel: they grapple with scientific knowledge or an adventure; or come to terms with their own nature. Some of them, through interacting with the environment, learn to cope with personal relationships.

Most of these books are set explicitly in South Africa. As successors to the 'Bushveld' prescribed works of the 1940s, they are a new way of expressing patriotism, of confirming the bond between South Africans and their country. The colourful local language and names for the creatures and plants express this sense of South Africanness. But now it is a patriotism that requires the conservation, rather than the exploitation, of the country.

Short works of fiction for children cannot of course be expected to reflect the full range and complexity of environmental conservation issues. If there is one significant issue on which they are silent, it is the involvement of the black population, the 'new players' referred to by Huntley in the passage quoted at the beginning of this chapter. As we have seen, hunters and conservationists have in the past all impinged upon the lives of the indigenous population without contemplating the moral, sociological, economic and political consequences. Yet among the many topics on which these books seek to raise the level of awareness of their readers, this impact features only in the mature novel *A Deadly Presence*. When one considers that quite a few modern children's books deal with various social issues in South Africa, this particular silence is all the more noticeable and to be regretted.

As a contrast to these ahistorical and apolitical novels, I turn, therefore, in the next chapter, to an historical novelist, Jenny Seed, and follow that by looking, in the last chapter, at modern children's novels that are politically aware.

NOTES

1. J. Stevenson-Hamilton, 'Foreword,' in *Our South African National Parks*, Cape Town: United Tobacco Company, 1940, iv.
2. Brian Huntley, 'Rotating the cube,' in *Rotating the Cube: Environmental Strategies for the 1990s*, ed. Graham Howe, Durban: Department of Geographical and Environmental Sciences and Indicator Project South Africa, University of Natal, 1990, 112, 115.
3. A.J. Clacherty, 'Towards an environmental education programme for the training of primary school teachers,' unpublished MSc dissertation, Cape Town: University of Cape Town, 1988.
4. Ian Player, 'One earth,' in *Rotating the Cube*, 7.
5. Frank W.J. Opie, *The Outdoor Classroom*, Cape Town: Maskew Miller Longman, 1989, 9.
6. Geoffrey and Susan Jellicoe, *The Landscape of Man: Shaping the Environment from Prehistory to the Present Day*, revised second edition, London: Thames & Hudson, 1987, 378.
7. John M. Mackenzie, *The Empire of Nature: Hunting, Conservation and British Imperialism*, Manchester: Manchester University Press, 1988.
8. M. van Wyk Smith, *Grounds of Contest: a Survey of South African English Literature*, Cape Town: Juta, 1990, 55.
9. Hilda Grobler, 'Me Tarzan – you Jane: sex stereotyping in children's books,' in *Towards Understanding/Op Weg Na Begrip*, ed. Isabel Cilliers, Cape Town: Maskew Miller Longman, 1988, 139.
10. Peter Hunt,'Arthur Ransome's *Swallows and Amazons*: escape to a lost paradise,' in *Touchstones: Reflections on the Best in Children's Literature*, ed. Perry Nodelman, West Lafayette: Children's Literature Association, 1985, 223.
11. L.W. Lanham and C.A. Macdonald, *The Standard in South African English and its Social History*, Amsterdam: Groos, 1979, 83.
12. Edmund Leach, *Culture and Communication: the Logic by which Symbols are Connected*, London: Cambridge University Press, 1976, 34.
13. Leach, *Culture and Communication*.
14. Opie, *The Outdoor Classroom*, Prologue and 6-11.

CHAPTER FIVE

Liberal History

No lad, not wicked. This is war, and war is always a wicked thing.
(Warriors on the Hills *61*)

One might say that, given the revision of South African history that has taken place in recent years, it is a brave novelist who would set out to write for children a series of novels set in some of the most controversial episodes of that history: the arrival of Jan van Riebeeck, the arrival of the British settlers in 1820 and 1850, the wars of the Boer trekkers against the Ndebele and Zulus, Shaka's wars, the Border Wars of the Eastern Cape, the Battle of Spioenkop and the Sieges of Ladysmith and Mafikeng during the Second Anglo-Boer War, the Kimberley diamond rush and the gold rush.

These are the settings of the historical novels of Jenny Seed, who is moved by her liberal view of history and the urgings of Christian compassion to convey to her young readers through the personal story of individuals what she sees as both sides of the story, and to impress upon them how personal values can make a significant mark for good in the midst of great historical events over which the individual would seem to have little control. In keeping with her concern for objectivity, she bases her novels on meticulously accurate historical detail. Not only are the words and actions of historical leaders authentic, but even the adventures of her child characters are in some instances suggested by actual events, and the contexts of their lives are minutely recreated.

As one of South Africa's most prolific and widely published – and therefore, presumably, most widely read – English children's authors, Jenny Seed can be assumed to have had a considerable didactic impact on children since her first book was published in 1968. Her influence has reached more than only white English-speaking South Africans, since many of her earlier books were first published in England in the days when publishers would not take the risk of publishing children's books in South Africa (though they have subsequently been republished in South Africa), and her books have also been translated into other languages such as German. Most notably, all her books are translated into Afrikaans, so that she may also be regarded as a prolific Afrikaans author. It is difficult to estimate what her black readership is, but it is probably very small. Since the only adult author to rival her historical scope is Stuart Cloete, Seed's works occupy an exceptional place in forming the historical sensibilities of white South Africans.

Although a number of other South African historical novels for children exist, none of them has achieved significant status, and no single author has produced the volume of work that Seed has. Her entire oeuvre of some forty books covers a wider range than the seventeen which constitute her historical fiction, but the rest are for younger readers and will not be discussed here. Even the historical novels are aimed at various age groups, ranging from seven or eight-year-olds to mid-teenagers, and have to be judged on different grounds – the ones for younger readers being less concerned to examine the nature of the historical circumstances in which the child characters find themselves. The first of the seventeen to be published was *The Voice of the Great Elephant*, in 1968, but it was not the first she wrote, that being *The Red Dust Soldiers*, which was eventually published in 1972.[1]

Although she can be criticised for her stilted style, slow-moving plots and the similarity of the plots and themes in many of her books, Jenny Seed has won critical recognition: in 1983 *The New Fire* gained an Honourable Mention for the Percy FitzPatrick Award, South Africa's senior award for English children's literature, and in 1987 *Place Among the Stones* was the first English book to be awarded the prestigious Afrikaans MER Prize for Children's Literature. Significantly, both these awards went to books that specifically confront issues of racial conflict: *The New Fire* deals with the persecution of the San, and *Place Among the Stones* deals with British prejudice towards the Boers in the Second Anglo-Boer War.

Seed's approach to controversial issues is to try to be impartial over the historical forces that impelled people. She emphasises the necessity of decent and fair behaviour and does not scruple to show the evil consequences of people's actions, both as individuals and collectively. In some of her weightier books, matters of state, often quoted directly from historical records, are related in some detail. In her concern to convey this information she sometimes assigns speeches to characters and historical figures such as Boer leaders in a decidedly awkward form of exposition which must become tedious to her young readers. The opening pages of *The Broken Spear* contain long speeches, prayers and lessons by Retief and others on leaving Egypt and entering the promised land, as a preamble to the Trekkers' crossing the Drakensberg into Natal. Similarly, when the Trekkers cross the Orange River in *The Unknown Land*, 'One of the women exclaimed, "Now we are really free. We are across the border. Never again shall we return to the Cape and the British officials and their laws!" ' (12), and many debates and religious services follow, in which the arguments for and against, and the consequences of, invading Mzilikazi's country are expounded. Hendrik Potgieter warns, 'If you cross the river he will be angry and think that we have come to steal his land' (19), and later Oom Jan asks, 'We came into his country without asking his permission and have been shooting his game. Do you call that nothing?' (28). In *Strangers in the Land* a man gives the new settlers information that sounds as though it comes straight from a school text book: 'In the April of 1819 thousands of Xhosa warriors invaded the colony. Without warning they poured across the Great Fish River and attacked the Boers who were farming here' (44).

Sometimes she puts historical exposition in prefaces and footnotes, though she has shortened earlier expositions in subsequent revised editions and reduced their use in her more recent books. Her revisions also show signs of attempts to moderate some of the more controversial material of earlier books. When *The Great Thirst*, first published in England in 1971, was extensively revised for the 1985 South African edition, a notable excision was Jonker Afrikaner's account of the cruel Boer farmer for whom he had worked. In the earlier edition he was named – Piet Pienaar – and Jonker described 'how he beat his servants with a sjambok' and 'would not even read to us out of the Book of the white man which told about God' (99-100) (though this was ameliorated by a footnote which explained rather lamely that he was an exception). She also uses prefaces to explain that the plots for some of her novels – *Gold Dust, The Red Dust Soldiers, The Spy Hill* – were suggested by actual incidents and by original documents which she uncovered, and to explain that her historical background is accurate, which indeed it is

Woven into her narratives are details like the actual wording of Baden-Powell's famous bulletin board notice of warning to spies (*Place Among the Stones*). An actual remark which Col. Thorneycroft made to Winston Churchill on Spioenkop is 'overheard' by the boy hero, Paul (*The Spy Hill*). M.C. Martin has pointed out that the first chapter of *The Prince of the Bay* follows closely the description of Zulu life in the chapter 'Daily life in Arcady' in Bryant's *The Zulu People*.[2] This kind of information is better integrated into the narrative than the political debate, although it is also sometimes stilted or implausibly provided: for example, the young Paul on Spioenkop overhears a Boer giving a detailed exposition of the Boer armaments to a friend, and during a bombardment on Mafikeng the mother explains to the grandmother why the baby is crying: ' "He's afraid of Big Ben. He knows that the big Boer gun usually fires its final shot of the day about now" ' (*Place Among the Stones* 9) – as if Grandmother needed the gloss on 'Big Ben'!

In her efforts to give readers a 'balanced' view of South African history, Jenny Seed encounters the difficulty facing authors of historical fiction, especially children's fiction, that the protagonists have a restricted point of view which, furthermore, has to be authentic to the character's time and place. How to give a Voortrekker boy an understanding of the point of view of the Zulus whose land his people are invading? One way that she has handled this is to vary the central characters of her books to cover different racial and cultural groups. The one major attack on her work to have been published was an ill-informed entry in *Twentieth Century Children's Writers* by Nancy J. Schmidt,[3] which accused her

112

of a limited, European perception of South African history, concentrating on the Boers. However, as Jay Heale has pointed out in a response to Schmidt,[4] this is far from the truth. A breakdown of the seventeen historical novels gives the background of the child protagonists as follows: six English-speaking, two half English/half Afrikaans and four Dutch/Afrikaans-speaking whites; three Africans; one San and one Nama. In addition, many of her other stories have black central characters, ranging from noble mythical figures to modern children. White children reading them will encounter black people portrayed without patronage.

Because of the limitations imposed by the restricted point of view of the characters, the stories have to concentrate on the personal experiences of people involved in historical events. This has the advantage of enabling Seed to show that everyone is a victim of historical circumstance but that individuals can, in the sphere of their own lives, behave honourably and with compassion towards their fellows. Despite her attempts to give the immediate reasons lying behind particular episodes, such as Jan van Riebeeck's establishment of the first Dutch settlement at the Cape, the importation of the 1820 British settlers, the Boer migrations to the interior known as the Great Trek, and the dispossession of the indigenous peoples of their land, Seed implies that the march of history is inevitable. True, these events did happen, and she cannot pretend otherwise, but one does gain a sense that she does not question their inevitability. This is particularly to be seen in the pleasure with which she describes the industry of the British settlers in creating order and applying their Protestant work ethic to the task of making themselves self-sufficient in the new land (*Warriors on the Hills*, *Strangers in the Land*, *The Year One*). But the pressure for European emigration to South Africa is accepted as given, in these books and in *The Far-away Valley*, which describes Van Riebeeck's arrival.

In her books, the excesses of human cruelty that accompanied the movement of peoples are not – cannot – be explained. In three novels, *The Voice of the Great Elephant*, *The Prince of the Bay*, and *Vengeance of the Zulu King*, she gives a conventional account of Shaka's reign as one of cruelty and havoc on a vast scale, explicable only in terms of the traditional powers of the monarch and the human foibles of Shaka and those who plotted to overthrow him. The gross atrocities that occur during wars are explicable only as a madness which afflicts even the best people.

This perception is embodied in the personal story of the hero of *The Great Thirst*, a Nama boy named Garib. From the time of his father's murder by the Herero leader, Kahitjene (who was, incidentally, an historical figure), Garib nurses his hatred and determination to be avenged. This hatred helps him overcome his revulsion at the massacres in which he is compelled to participate, but at the end he cannot bring himself to kill his enemy:

> *When still a child he had discovered that strange thing that when one hurt another one might feel the wound in one's own body. Now he found that hatred too might reflect back on the one who hated. (125)*

The Great Thirst epitomises Seed's attempts to be balanced. It describes a period of great upheaval in Namibia in the early nineteenth century when the Oorlam leader, Jonker Afrikaner, subjugated the Nama, settled Windhoek and alternately fought and formed alliances with Herero factions. She describes the good and the bad side of the Oorlam, the Hereros and the white missionaries and traders, but ultimately makes no overt historical judgements, ascribing their actions to the whims of human nature and the inevitability of certain forms of human behaviour. From the confusing story of the fluctuations of peace and war, the young reader may learn the lesson of history that nobody is entirely good or bad. The white men bring Christianity, but also arms, alcohol and greed. Missionaries who are not particularly effective eventually give up and leave Windhoek. Nor do the Christians have the monopoly on religion – Garib decides that 'There was only one God. There was one wisdom which all men shared' (141). Further lessons to be found in the story are that good leaders might resort to treachery to protect their people, that war can get out of hand and lead to atrocities, and so on.

Seed's preference is always for order and good government. She often gives examples of how traditional Zulu society operated with orderliness and justice – 'For it was not the way of the people to decide on matters before all arguments had been weighed and each man had spoken out as it was his right to do' (*The Prince of the Bay* 151). It is just unfortunate, she implies, that the system could not stand up to Shaka's capriciousness. Perhaps it is Seed's satisfaction at seeing the land occupied by peaceful Zulu villages, or farmed by industrious settlers, that excludes from her work any nostalgia for a pristine Africa from which man was absent. She realistically accepts that people occupied South Africa long before the Europeans arrived. Hence her work is atypical of so much historical fiction which portrays 'darkest Africa' as a place to be feared, or as a place to be raped. It is consistent, therefore, that she does not take an extreme environmentalist position, deploring the destruction of the environment and wildlife. She has only one episode with this theme – an elephant hunt in *Strangers in the Land*, described with gruesome detail, which she emphasises was an illegal act by ivory hunters. Perhaps environmental conservation is too modern a concept to be consonant with her view of Africa. When asked in an interview, 'Have you any plans to come closer to our time?' she replied, '... I've tried to think of it, but I feel absolutely out of touch. I think that one would have to be a person of the time, and I don't think I am.'[5] (Though this disclaimer does not account for her post-colonial liberal historicism.)

She ignores the implications of the exploitation of the country's mineral resources through the advent of large scale capitalism, although mining provides the background to two of her novels. *Canvas City* is set in Kimberley during the diamond rush, and *Gold Dust* is set in Pilgrim's Rest soon after the discovery of gold. The themes of both novels are restricted to the unpleasant effects of greed on people: the filthy mining camps, the brutalised behaviour. Though it is only a plot device, it is perhaps significant that the crooks in *Canvas City* steal diamonds, for, as Michael Rice has pointed out,[6] IDB (illicit diamond buying) was one of the most heinous crimes in the eyes of profit-minded nineteenth century colonisers, as the plots of many early novels set in South Africa make clear; and Seed accepts this judgement. Her resolution in both these stories is for the children's families to come to their senses, reject the feverish greed of the miners, and leave the diggings to go farming (which they have fortunately now made enough money to afford). Her march of history stops short of the industrialisation and urbanisation of South Africa.

Only twice do Seed's plots conclude with the hopelessness of the actual historical record. In *The Broken Spear* the Afrikaans boy, Dirk, enjoys a short-lived friendship with a Zulu boy, Tuntu, but in the final horror of the slaughter at Blood River, he finds

Tuntu's body. No other resolution is possible. Seed assigns to Dirk a final thought, which has not yet been fulfilled: 'If all the bloodshed were not to be merely useless destruction, he and the others would have to work to make this the place they had prayed it would be' (143). In spite of its title, *The New Fire* leaves the reader with a sense of the pathos and hopelessness of the fate of the San. After white farmers have attacked the Bushmen in retaliation for the theft of their sheep, and kidnapped a little girl to make her a servant, as was their practice, the grandfather leads the remnants of the little band further into the interior. Their courage and love are a powerful testimony to the human spirit, but we know their case is hopeless. As the grandfather says,

> *It is the strangers who did wrong!... First it was the black people, then the brown people, then the white people ... All people know that the animals belong to the Great Spirit who made them, and no Bushman will kill more than he needs for meat. But the strangers kill and kill until there is no game left ... (21)*

With the hindsight of history, Seed is able to make the plot of her major novel on the conflict between Boer and Brit, *Place Among the Stones*, reflect a more confident note of resolution. Rice points out that the theme of reconciliation emerged in Boer War fiction rather late – no doubt, when this reconciliation became a reality, decades later.[7] At the end of her story, the English-speaking Johnny sufficiently overcomes his antipathy towards the Boer youth, Jannie, to pass on Jannie's message to his sister that he will be back after the war, and we may assume that Jannie and the English-speaking girl will marry. It is this reconciliation, and the sympathetic portrayal of the Boers, that probably led to the unprecedented award of the Afrikaans prize for the book.

The need for understanding and communication is a common theme in modern South African children's books, but it did not become urgent in Seed's works until recently. Her 1972 novel, *The Broken Spear*, does feature the friendship between Dirk and Tuntu, who meet when Tuntu's family care for Dirk until he has recovered from a fall. Admittedly the boys cannot speak each other's language, but apart from mentioning that they swim together with a group of boys, no detail is given of their time together which might explain how they become attached. Only in Seed's last two books published in 1987 is communication between cultures the focus. In *Place Among the Stones* we have Johnny's wrestling with his prejudice against Afrikaners, and in *The Far-away Valley*, a short, illustrated book for young children, the little Dutch boy and the Khoekhoen boy shyly accept each other as human beings in a brief encounter:

> *It suddenly occurred to Willem that he must seem as strange and different to this boy as the boy seemed to him ... Wanting to respond in some way, Willem stretched out his hand to touch the boy's arm. At once the beachranger gasped and drew back as if he, too, was afraid. Willem wondered if he would run away but he did not ... They looked into each other's eyes and they both smiled as if they had shared a discovery. It was almost as if they had spoken to one another. (28)*

The illustrations by Joan Rankin, which reflect the Edenic innocence of this scene, won for her the First Prize in the prestigious Daan Retief Publishers Competition for Book Illustrators in 1987.

Whether she is presenting people through the eyes of the protagonist or through her narrative, Seed obviously tries to exclude any racist perceptions which would probably have been historically accurate for the time. At a simple level this shows in her concern for terminology and language usage, even though it means breaking with her usually meticulous authenticity. Where whites would have used other epithets, her characters refer to black people as 'tribesmen', 'the Baralong' and 'black men'. The Khoekhoen boy is called a 'beachranger' (her own translation of the term 'strandloper'), a name which by reason of its novelty is neutral. Seed herself originally wrote Zulu names and words casually, spelling them as she liked, but in revised editions correct Zulu orthography has been substituted: Ntombi for Tombi, Khulumi for Kulumi, the royal greeting 'bayede' for 'bayete', and so on. In earlier works she usually gave a translation of non-English words, directly in the text, or in a footnote, or indirectly, as in ' "Sakubona!" Mbaya said at last. "We have seen you, man of Zulu" ' (*Voice of the Great Elephant* 8); but in later works she leaves snatches of dialogue in the original, for the reader to figure out.

In novels where we know that the entire action must have taken place in another language, she adapts the English to echo the original idiom – a technique for which she has been criticised by reviewers, for it does sound stilted. King Shaka says,

> *Is it not the custom of my men, Great Headman, to feed themselves when they live at the king's house?... Shall the king feed the people then?... Know this then, I do not forget my promises.*
> (Voice of the Great Elephant *35*)

She is fond of using this style in her books about Zulus to suggest, by indirect quotation in her narrative, what 'the people' are thinking: 'And if anyone noticed that he spoke but little they thought nothing of it, for was it not right that one who had no family should have a voice that was small?' (*The Prince of the Bay* 98). The effect of giving an 'Afrikaans' flavour to her Afrikaans speakers is similar to that of two classic South African writers, Pauline Smith and Herman Charles Bosman. She even has a Boer repeating a well-known Afrikaans proverb: 'Yes, tell them that even the old ox at the back comes at last into the kraal' (*The Spy Hill* 21).

Seed breaks down her readers' culture-bound preconceptions by presenting the variety of South Africa's peoples through many points of view. For example, the Nama describe Western clothing as 'clothing like the scum on stagnant water' (*The Great Thirst* 86). A Zulu boy is amazed to see that white men put

> *some [boxes] even upon the backs of oxen, which was astonishing to those who stood watching, for what man had ever used the precious cattle to carry burdens when there were wives or boys to do the work?*
> (The Prince of the Bay 56-57)

And the Boers who reach Port Natal find the Englishmen dressed in Zulu loin cloths, and with black families (*The Broken Spear*). *The Red Dust Soldiers* contains a warm portrayal of a Boer family who care for the little English boy who wanders across the lines during the siege of Ladysmith. The British in the two sieges are often shown to be pompous and self-righteous: 'Father had always tried to teach him to be brave as an Englishman should be' *(The*

Red Dust Soldiers 26). The reader is left in no doubt that the Mafikeng priest who preaches about the Boers' 'spiritual wickedness' is guilty of reprehensible bigotry, as bad as that of the women Johnny overhears gossiping cruelly about his Afrikaans mother *(Place Among the Stones)*.

A most effective shift in point of view is achieved when Seed uses a Zulu centre of consciousness to evoke the quality of traditional Zulu life. The opening pages of *The Prince of the Bay* introduce the reader to this world through the senses of the Zulu boy as he wakes in his hut – descriptive writing that Seed has not matched in subsequent works:

> *He lifted his head from his wooden headrest ... In the fireplace in the centre one tiny spark still glowed ... silence except for the scurrying of the hut beetles as they moved about in the big clay pots ... the familiar odours of his mother's hut, which, heightened by the dampness of dawn, came up to him strongly and sweetly from the clean dung floor. There was the sharp scent of the reeds of the sleeping mats and the tang of wood-smoke and the odours of earth and clay pots and drying hides and also the sour-sweet smell of fermenting beer ... (6)*

The Zulu world picture is shown to be consistent and logical:

> *Were not all things which people made rounded so that they satisfied the hands and eye of the one who worked? The huts, the kraals, the pots and dishes, the baskets, and the black rings of wax men wore upon their heads were all round. And did not the birds and the beasts know this roundness also so that even the scorned nest of the swallow was a rounded tunnel of mud? (35)*

Her Zulu novels are filled with picturesque imagery, again not to be found in later books. Like a leitmotiv, those who have died at Shaka's hands are said to have 'eaten earth'. Descriptive similes mingle with more complex metaphors: 'Where the open hillsides had lain like old dogs in the sun, brown and gold with the winter drought' (34); and

> *As the hot days of summer sometimes stretch out into the*

119

> *winter, and the heat lingers on even when the time for frost*
> *has come, Bongiseni felt that he was living on, spared from*
> *death for a while, in a season that was already past. (52)*

And again in *Voice of the Great Elephant*: 'As the grass grows thin
against a huge mountain, he had almost ceased to live because of
the shadow of the Great Elephant' (69).

These early novels are not only lyrical but contain prose of
powerful rhythm, which helps to explain the fearsomeness and incredible courage of the massed Zulu warriors:

> *Vika found that his feet were stamping. He too wanted to*
> *rush forward and dance ... His arms and legs felt as*
> *strong as a man's. As strong as the mightiest warrior's. A*
> *madness seemed to come over him so that no thought of*
> *fear remained. He yearned to grasp the plumes from the*
> *heads of those near him and place them on his own.*
> (Voice of the Great Elephant *45*)

This vigorous portrayal of what it was like to be a Zulu in the
nineteenth century is inexplicably contradicted by stereotypes of
blacks as seen through the eyes of whites in some of Seed's other
novels. In an early work, a servant danced and jumped around,
'grinned and rolled his eyes' (*Canvas City* 116), and the caricature
persists: in *Warriors on the Hills* the blacks had always been 'gay
and friendly' (111). *The Spy Hill* perpetuates the image to be found
in so many novels about South Africa, of the faithful retainer who
is treated in a kindly way, as though he is rather simple. Kobus,
the elderly servant, exclaims, 'Ai! We have come a long way. A
lo...ng way!' (sic), whereupon 'Paul's father gave an amused
chuckle, then called softly to someone to give the old man refresh-
ments' (23). It is in keeping with this relationship that the white
boy, Paul, risks his life to rescue Kobus from the battlefield, after
Kobus is shot while fetching water for him.

While the conflict between whites and the independent black
nations is a major theme which Seed explores, she does not pursue
the contentious issue of the place and fate of the black servants
and fighters who were loyal to the whites. For example, although
the part played by blacks in the defence of Mafikeng and their
treatment by Baden-Powell are currently central to interest in the

siege, they remain peripheral to her story, *Place Among the Stones*. However, they are not entirely ignored: 'If it had not been for the locusts, people said, many more of the black people would have died of hunger' (54), and the notorious execution of a black 'spy' is included.

Literary critics often point out how South African literature reflects the marginalisation of blacks, women and children, and it is interesting to see how Seed handles these groups. After all, she is herself marginalised – a woman writer, and on top of that, a writer for children, which is an occupation of little status in the country. (Significantly, there are very few male children's writers in South Africa, certainly none with the status of Seed and Marguerite Poland.) In two of her novels, *The Great Thirst* and *The Broken Spear*, she mentions ill-treatment of black servants by Boers, and in the latter it is explicitly equated with the treatment of a white child. The boy, Dirk, is an orphan who has to work as a servant for his foster-father and is harshly treated and whipped by him. Early in the novel, Dirk hears a Boer giving his reasons for leaving the Cape: 'A Christian may not even correct his Hottentots with a beating without risking a case in the law courts' (2). Another white child who is abused in his capacity as a servant is Jeremiah of *Strangers in the Land*, apprenticed to a drunken master with whom he travels from England. We are not spared details of his maltreatment, such as his being beaten over the head with a riding crop. This is the only fictional account of which I am aware of the plight of the British orphans who were sent to South Africa with the 1820 Settlers and in subsequent years. By 1840, when there were some 800 white apprentice boys in South Africa, rumours of their maltreatment had become so rife that at the request of the Children's Friend Society, which sponsored their emigration, Lord John Russell, then Colonial Secretary, instructed Sir George Napier, Governor of the Cape Colony, to institute an inquiry. Happily, extensive investigations by four magistrates found that 'the apprehensions of the Society were in a great measure groundless'.[8]

Most of the protagonists in Seed's stories are boys. This may be because, in the periods about which she writes, girls were too domesticated to have the freedom to enjoy the adventures that were open to boys in a frontier society. Two successful writers of historical novels for children, Hester Burton and Rosemary Sutcliff, have admitted that their settings give opportunities for 'robust, exciting stories' of 'young people thrown into some terrible predicament or danger and scrambling out of it unaided' and that in earlier times 'more was demanded of youngsters – a boy of fourteen could play a man's part'.[9] Certainly, Seed is better at writing about action than domesticity, and she has confirmed that in this she has been influenced by other historical children's writers. She said in an interview, 'I was very influenced by Henry Treece because of his boldness; to feel that I could write almost in an adult fashion for children, not writing down at all, and not worrying too much about the blood and thunder'. Defending her inclusion of horrifying detail, she said, 'Well, it was true, it did happen, and I think reality is harsh, but one can manage to take it if it is not sadistic or twisted.'[10] It is typical of these details that the twelve-year-old Paul, alone at night on the field of Spioenkop, is surrounded by 'the groaning of hundreds of wounded and dying Tommies' and he touches a corpse *(The Spy Hill* 53); and in the opening of *Place Among the Stones*, when Johnny attends a mass burial and the bodies are carried past him in canvas bags, 'he was aware suddenly of a strange airless odour coming from them' (2). Yet her boys are not tough young heroes. More often they are insecure and bungling and very dominated by their fathers. They collapse, they crash wagons, they get lost. Richard of *The Policeman's Button* makes an utter fool of himself in front of the Natal Mounted Police by getting lost just outside his own backyard. However, they usually come up trumps, to their own surprise, when put to the test.

Seed's girls are usually insignificant, They stay at home with mother and defer to their brothers' superior knowledge. However, there are signs that she is moving towards portraying a more positive role for women. Only three books have girl protagonists and of those it is only in the early work, *Canvas City*, that the girl is able to find fulfilment in her feminine role. Maggie does not work on the diamond diggings like her father and brother, but she helps her mother keep the family together and decent in the midst of the dirt and frenzy. Seed's next heroine rebels against a passive role. *The Year One* begins as though it is the story of eleven-year-old Edward, but after a few pages we realise that his eight-year-old sister, Alice, is actually the central character, her ambition being to emulate her brother and father – 'She wished with all her heart she could be brave enough to do something new also' (45). Her wish is granted: while minding the baby she is able to drive off an aggressive monkey.

In an obvious progression, the last of the girl heroines has a masculine job to do. In *Gold Dust*, Katy is the oldest child and has to work. We first meet her leading a team of oxen, normally a task for black boys, and we are told that 'Pappie had taught her a few words from their Dutch Bible, but because she was a girl, and because she was needed on the farm to help her father, her parents had not sent her to school' (13). The miners call her 'Crowbar Kate'. Tomboys in children's fiction are usually simply the opposite side of the coin to stereotypes of femininity – they usually give up their tomboyishness in the end, so that the aberration proves the rule – but as usual Seed tries to give a balanced picture, in this case affirming both Katy's masculine usefulness and her femininity. Although Katy 'did not really want to be a boy' (51), through her strength she is able to fetch help for a miner who has gone down with malaria. The miner is Tom, a young teacher, with whom she has a friendship that verges on sexual attraction. When they part he gives her a piece of filigree gold with a thank-you note, to 'the bravest, most intelligent and most beautiful lady on the diggings', and she reflects that she really enjoyed her time as a miner.

Seed's women are what the girls in her novels will grow up to be – stoic supporters of their husbands, hard working, engaged in child-bearing and child-minding, and loading the guns for the men when they are attacked. Their neutral role is epitomised by the historically accurate depiction of the women's camp, situated in no-man's land outside Ladysmith, which the little boy of *The Red Dust Soldiers* symbolically leaves in order to join the men under fire in the town. Most memorably, women are the innocent sufferers, whether their suffering is described in the bathos of the passing remark, 'Soon he became accustomed to it – the salt beef and the bitter water and the crowded decks and the children dying almost every week and being buried at sea' *(Strangers in the Land* 12), or in the grim details of the Blaauwkrans massacre, with women and children screaming and their blood dripping under the wagon on to Dirk's arm *(The Broken Spear)*. (Notice that the suffering is seen through the eyes of males.) Only in a later work, *Place Among the Stones*, do we find a woman who is independent and pro-active. She is the boy protagonist's sister, a young nurse, who defiantly cultivates friendship with a wounded Boer prisoner.

Because Seed portrays her characters as part of historical processes over which they have little influence, she focusses interest on their personal – moral and psychological – struggles. These struggles are linked with the historical events and the incidents of the plot. In an interview, she has described her creative process:

> *Once I've realised that a child can be there, and there is sufficient action for a child to be involved in, then somehow the child, whether it's a boy or a girl, because there has to be a hero for a child to identify with, begins to take shape, and the character begins to form. The character and the plot form together, not the plot through the character, because the plot is already fixed and it has to be a character who can, through the plot, work out some character development in themselves.*[11]

Since her plots are adventurous and often set in violent times, the lessons that the children of her early novels learn deal, appropriately, with the nature of fear and courage, self-assertion, hatred, vengeance and forgiveness. Typically, Vika of *Voice of the Great Elephant* realises that

> *It was a comfort for him to know that he was not a coward, but he could never love war for he knew that battle only brought sadness and death and the courage of a warrior was a madness in the blood. (89)*

The psychological struggle within the children is to find an identity as they grow to maturity that does not depend on norms of violence, aggression and greed. Gradually her novels shift in interest to adolescents' relationships with their parents or other adults, and the tension lies in their bonding with, or rejection of, the adult, and the dilemma of whether to accept or reject the adult's values.

Some of her characters have an ideally close, warm relationship with their parents. Seed is particularly good at portraying the father/child relationship. However, there are some startling, moving accounts of defective relationships as well. The black boy of *Prince of the Bay*, whose life was saved by Henry Francis Fynn and who becomes his devoted servant, sees at the end that Fynn will remain a white man and they will drift apart. Dirk, the orphan of *The Broken Spear*, hates his brutal foster-father, and it is as part of his rejection of this man's values that Dirk questions his religion – 'It is not so. It is a lie. God is not here in this terrible country' – and comes finally even to reject hatred – 'He could not hate the Zulus' (131). From the age of twelve, Matthew, the English settler boy of *Strangers in the Land*, grows distant from his father. At the age of fourteen he rejects his father as a fool for depending on scriptural texts while their family's struggles to make a living off the land show no results. Using the device of an alter ego, the free-spirited Jeremiah, Seed has Matt run away from home on an impulse to join Jeremiah. But he becomes involved with illegal ivory hunters who, it is noted, do not follow the Boer tradition of holding family prayers. (Their leader has a 'narrow, foxy face' [103].) After Matt returns home to his forgiving parents, symbolically it is the candle that he lights to read the Bible that induces Jeremiah to come inside and join him in his home.

Strangers in the Land is not all that convincing as a psychological novel. Marina le Roux has justly pointed out how the characters are seen from the outside and their actions are not adequately motivated, and she also notes the clichés in the writing – 'a scarlet blush of shame', 'a shocked silence'.[12] Blemishes of this sort crop up in all the novels. A typical example of how clichés give an external view of a character occurs when Matt witnesses the slaughter of the elephants. The narrator does not tell us he was horrified, or even that he *felt* the horror; instead, his reactions are given at third remove: 'He was aware of a feeling of stunned horror' (115).

It seems that Seed was trying something new with this book – she has acknowledged that she had recently become a Christian when she wrote it, which suggests a new interest in moral issues.[13] In place of the calm imagery of her Zulu novels, she tries something more fanciful. When Jeremiah responds to Matt's candle and comes indoors, 'as he passed Matthew thought that he smelt of the wind and the cold night air, a wild free kind of smell' (155). The weakest aspect of the book is the unconvincing portrayal of the friendship between the two boys. As we have seen, Seed had the same trouble with a much earlier description of a friendship, in *The Broken Spear*. This perhaps explains why nearly all her child characters are loners, which is not a typical feature of children's books.

Seed returned to the novel of adolescence in *Place Among the Stones*, which has rightly been acclaimed, because here everything fits together. The inner conflicts of the boy reflect the themes of the war in which he is involved. With slight touches she conveys the distance between the boy and his father, resulting from the reserved Edwardian's difficulty in communicating with his thirteen-year-old son: he speaks to him in a 'brisk, slightly formal, slightly embarrassed tone' (4). Johnny is not able to confide in his father, distracted as the adult is by his work and war duties. However, the real conflict – and this is a new and daring one for Seed – is Johnny's rejection of his mother. She is Afrikaans, married to an Englishman, and now besieged in Mafikeng while her brother fights on the Boer side. Johnny believes that she is a Boer spy, and this far-fetched suspicion finds fertile ground in the young adolescent's natural rejection of maternal ties. And so his ambivalent feelings towards his parents reflect the dilemma of how he should feel about the war. All around him are calls to take a jingoistic attitude towards the Boers, yet his parents represent a different ethic. For a time he rejects them. Surely, in wartime when one aims to kill, his father should, like the other men, cheer a direct hit on the enemy? 'To be so decent and upright was not even honest, he thought resentfully' (38).

Here the alter ego is introduced explicitly, in the form of a Boer youth with the same name as his own, in its Afrikaans form – 'Jannie'. Johnny has to force himself not to admit that Jannie is a decent person who bears none of his prejudices. Johnny's conversion to a more conciliatory attitude is a result both of his experiences in the siege and of the tolerance of his parents. Reconciliation with his mother does not wipe out the hurt, but she kindly blames the rift on the war. His father's action in going to fetch him and walk home with him from the celebrations marking the Relief shows that they can be companions.

By focussing on the *angst* of individual characters, Jenny Seed is a white novelist of her time. Kenneth Parker has said that

> *One characteristic difference that continues to demarcate the writing of white South Africans from that of their black counterparts in the past quarter-century is that the former still concentrate upon individuals ... By contrast, for black*

*writers ... it is generally the whole community which re-
sists, challenges, the dominant ideology.*[14]

It is typical of the liberal vision to focus on the individual, as
Stephen Watson points out in his essays attacking white South African liberals. Seed's vision of the role of the individual in society
fits Watson's definition in many respects: 'Amongst the values
[liberalism] advocates, those of "reasonableness", "common-sense"
and "toleration" are invariably given heavy stress', and – he adds
to the list by quoting Lionel Trilling – ' "a ready if mild suspicion
of the profit motive, a belief in progress ..." '.[15]

Andreé-Jeanne Tötemeyer confirms that this is typical, not only
of Seed's writing, but of her contemporaries as well:

*Although South African youth books have become quite
progressive in recent years ... these themes concentrate
mainly on conflict-management at an inter-personal (mi-
cro-social) level, i.e. in the family, school and peer group.
It has, however, become imperative for authors to broaden
their perspective to include conflict managemen on the
macro-social level, i.e. towards peace and understanding
between groups in society at large.*[16]

Seed is a creature of her time, a time aptly defined by Stephen
Gray: 'For we are, and throughout the century have been, all of us,
suspended between African historical moments that should have
coincided: we are post-colonial beings, but still we are preindepen-
dent'.[17] Her view of South Africa's past is post-colonial, but it is
far from being a radical re-writing of history.

NOTES

1. Bon Gertz, 'Jenny Seed interviewed,' *The Cape Librarian*, March
1979, 5.
2. M.C. Martin, 'Jenny Seed's South African books,' *Libri Natales*,
July 1971, 14.
3. Nancy J. Schmidt, 'Jenny Seed,' in *Twentieth Century Children's
Writers*, ed. D.L. Kirkpatrick, Second Edition, New York: St Martin's
Press, 1985, 682. Reprinted in *Newsletter of the United States Board on*

Books for Young People, Fall 1986, 10.

4. Jay Heale, 'Response to Nancy Schmidt,' *Newsletter of the United States Board on Books for Young People*, Fall 1986, 9.

5. Gertz, 'Jenny Seed interviewed,' 5.

6. M.C. Rice, 'From Dolly Gray to Sarie Marais: a survey of fiction in English concerning the First and Second Anglo-Boer conflicts,' unpublished D Litt et Phil thesis, Johannesburg: Rand Afrikaans University, 1983.

7. Rice, 'From Dolly Gray to Sarie Marais,' 227.

8. Quoted in Gillian Wagner, *Children of the Empire*, London: Weidenfeld and Nicholson, 1982, 15.

9. Quoted in M. Sarah Smedman, 'Esther Forbes' *Johnny Tremain*: authentic history, classic fiction,' in *Touchstones. Reflections on the Best in Children's Literature*, ed. Perry Nodelman, West Lafayette: Children's Literature Association, 1985, 85.

10. Gertz, 'Jenny Seed interviewed,' 7.

11. Gertz, 'Jenny Seed interviewed,' 6.

12. Marina le Roux, 'Jenny Seed lewer een van die beste jeugboeke van die jaar,' *Die Burger*, 19 November 1987, 4.

13. Gertz, 'Jenny Seed interviewed,' 6.

14. Kenneth Parker, 'Imagined revolution: Nadine Gordimer's *A Sport of Nature*,' in *Women and Writing in South Africa: A Critical Anthology*, ed. Cherry Clayton, Johannesburg: Heinemann, 1989, 213.

15. Stephen Watson, 'Recent white South African poetry and the language of liberalism,' in *Publisher/Writer/Reader: Sociology of Southern African Literature*, ed. Susan Gardner, Johannesburg, University of the Witwatersrand, 1986, 202.

16. Andreé-Jeanne Tötemeyer, 'Towards interracial understanding through South African children's and youth literature,' in *Towards Understanding/Op Weg na Begrip: Children's Literature for Southern Africa*, ed. Isabel Cilliers, Cape Town: Maskew Miller Longman, 1988,87.

17. Stephen Gray, 'A working position,' in *Momentum: On Recent South African Writing*, ed. M.J. Daymond, J.U. Jacobs and M. Lenta, Pietermaritzburg: University of Natal Press, 1984, 35.

CHAPTER SIX

Race and Social Issues

Being 14 didn't help you understand, really.
(Janet Smith, Streams to Rivers*)*

When the father of thirteen-year-old Tom Finnaughty, destined to become the poacher-bashing hero of Dale Kenmuir's wildlife adventures, enters his son's bedroom in Haslemere, Surrey, to reprimand him for his poor school report,

> *Against one wall he saw a bookshelf with an untidy sprawl of books, prominent among them* Jock of the Bushveld, *several hunting books by Courtney Selous, and a selection of novels by Rider Haggard.* The Insect World of J. Henri Fabre *lay on a small desk near the window, alongside a junior microscope, and open on the bed was Wolhuter's* Memories of a Game Ranger.
> *(*Dry Bones Rattling 2*)*

In 1976, little Andre of lower Woodstock, Cape Town, helps his neighbour, Mrs Ebrahim, bury her son Yusuf's books in the garden before the police raid the house:

> *Some of the books slid out of the carrier bag as he dug. He glanced at the titles:* An African Bourgeoisie, The Road to

Wigan Pier, Chaos or Community, The Failure of American Liberalism.
(Ann Harries, The Sound of the Gora *102)*

The children's books from which these episodes come, an archetypal Bushveld adventure and a story of child political activists, represent two of the three main streams of English children's and youth fiction in South Africa of the 1980s and early 1990s. We have looked at the first of these themes, the relationship of people with their natural environment, in Chapters Three and Four; in Chapter Five we looked at a writer on the second theme, the history of this country; in this chapter we turn to the theme of the relationships between people in modern South Africa.

The children's uprising of 1976 marked the liberation of South African English children's books from a taboo on matters of race and politics.

Not that race had been absent from them before then; earlier books simply reflected the status quo and the racial attitudes that predominated among whites at the time. *Jock of the Bushveld*, for example, contains terminology and a description of the episode of Jock's rout of the Shangaan miners that today read as gross racism.

The involvement of children in political activism that began in 1976 provided material for realistic plots on this new theme, and prompted writers to make race and contemporary social issues the focus of children's books instead of the unmarked background. Three youth novels, in fact, are set in the events of 1976: *Go well, Stay well*, by Toeckey Jones (1979), *The Sound of the Gora* by Ann Harries (1980), and *The Day of the Kugel* by Barbara Ludman (1989).

As the pace of political reform has increased and South African society has become freer, more and more children's and youth novels on these themes have been published, exploiting the greater tolerance of what may be published and children may read. Their plots, too, explore the potential that a more open society offers for young people to meet and learn about their fellows who have been distanced from them until now by apartheid.

A fresh perspective

Of the two dozen or more books that concentrate on race and social issues, all have children or teenagers as protagonists, and – unlike the fiction on the environmental theme or Jenny Seed's historical novels – a significant number are told wholly or in part in the first person, sometimes in the form of a diary. Even when narrated in the third person, the books are generally successful at realising a single, unique centre of consciousness, though this genre also has its share of inept, amateurish writing and poor narrative technique.

We can note here that on the whole, when the books are illustrated, the illustrations, especially of people, are usually excruciatingly crude. Sometimes they are also inaccurate. The text of *Borderline* by Ann Dymond, for example, makes much of the fact that the children wear jeans, but the illustrator shows the boys in shorts and the girl in a dress.

By concentrating on one or two young people as the centres of consciousness in a novel, the authors explore the impact on their youthful sensitivities of the events and human relationships that they experience. But there is a difference between the way these modern youngsters react to the world around them and the way Jenny Seed's historical characters do. The difference lies both in the writers' perspicacious understanding of the difference between a child of the past and a child of today, and in the use that the writers want to make of their characters. A look at some of the modern protagonists will illustrate this.

Charlie is the kid sister who tells the story of *The Kayaboeties* (the second, and much better, book by Elana Bregin, author of *Warrior of Wilderness*). Charlie, her brother, his friends and a black boy whom they meet form a band that practises in the vacant servant's quarters, or 'kaya', at a friend's house. She is a chatterbox who likes to comment on what she sees around her, such as the kaya:

> It wasn't my favourite place in the world. Firstly, it didn't smell too good on account of the blocked toilet next door and secondly, it was a pretty ugly place, even for a kaya: dark and small and stuffy – like a jail, I thought – with a concrete floor and tiny windows and walls so patched with

131

> *damp and mildew that there was hardly any paint left on them ... I always found it really depressing to think of anyone actually having to live in such a hole. (2)*

Charlie is firmly against racial prejudice, and makes shrewd observations about it in other people. Quoting one of the boys as saying 'Bloody cheeky coon – I'll soon sort him out,' she remarks, 'He gets that kind of talk from his father' (22), and she says, 'Our parents were a lot more decent about black people than Pecker's were, but only up to a point. They still had a lot of old-fashioned ideas to get rid of' (71). Here, then, is the first characteristic of the modern child: pert and outspoken, quick to observe and to report her observations.

Pert children also ask questions. In *Borderline*, Roger, who is also the youngest of a group, wants to know why somebody accused of being an 'agitator' had to leave the country: 'Why were they chasing him because he can read and write and make speeches?' (12) By the time they become teenagers, encounters with a wider circle of people and concomitantly with ideas and issues, provoke deeper questions. Corina, the central character of Dianne Hofmeyr's *A Sudden Summer* (her first novel, written before *When Whales go Free*) is drawn, out of human interest, to approach a girl whom she sees hiding with two younger children in the dunes near Gordon's Bay. The living conditions of black and so-called coloured people have already had a vague place in her consciousness as she reads headlines about Crossroads and she is prompted, when she see coloured people getting off her bus to go home, to wonder what it is like to have no electricity; but the personal encounter with the homeless children leads her to serious questioning of the plight of the homeless and the political background to forced removals.

The questions that are asked are complex and philosophical. In book after book the young people puzzle over race: why are there different races; does that make people different; should it make any difference to the way they behave towards each other? In *Down Street* by Lawrence Bransby, when a white teenager, Ted, makes friends with coloured Christina, the sensational emphasis that society gives to their racial difference leads them to debate whether racial prejudice is instinctive or learnt. Michelle, in *Streams to Rivers* by Janet Smith, has grown up in a 'liberal' family (her father edits *Think!* magazine), but it is only when she begins a serious friendship with a black boy that she starts trying to understand history, current affairs and the complexities of racial behaviour in South Africa. The most complete education in South African current affairs is that of the American teenager, also a Michelle, who, in Barbara Ludman's *Day of the Kugel*, arrives in the country in 1976 and sets out, like her namesake, to interpret the events that impinge on her life. Using a plot device similar to that of Nadine Gordimer's *A World of Strangers*, Ludman has the foreigner befriend both wealthy, complacent whites and black and white radicals, from whom she gains different perspectives.

What these writers are doing, therefore, is using the point of view of innocent children, ignorant white teenagers or a visiting young American to present a fresh view of South Africa, stripped of adult cant. The use of an ingénue for this purpose is not new in South African literature: these books follow what Margaret Lenta calls 'a distinguished line of Southern African fiction which begins with Gordimer's *The Lying Days* (1953) and Lessing's *Martha Quest* (1965).'[1] Going back a lot further, we can think also of *The Diary of Iris Vaughan*.

Through empathising with white characters, white readers can sense the hurt caused by apartheid, though they cannot realise the full depths of what it has inflicted. That white South Africans can grow up so ignorant of the history and ramifications of apartheid and its effects on the daily lives of people classified as 'non-white' is in itself part of the writers' commentary on South African society. Their didactic thrust is to teach young readers a view of South African history and current affairs that is not white-centred, to experience through the protagonists a different paradigm of human relations, and share with them growth in formulating a personal credo to direct their lives. In this endeavour, the writers are, of course, constrained by the juvenile perspective to limit their exploration of history and politics to what the young protagonists might be expected to understand, and to limit their portrayal of personal and social experience to what is, in South Africa, thought appropriate for young reading.

The Sound of the Gora by Ann Harries (1980) is a key text in conveying an altered perspective. It uses the device of alternating episodes from 1976 and from 1800 to support the revisionist view of history called for by a young Black Consciousness orator,

Yusuf. As the modern Andre's father says, 'They [black children] have learnt about themselves through the eyes of their white masters over the ages; now they must see themselves as the children of Africa' (86). Speeches by Yusuf alternate with a moving account of Boers shooting San and turning their children into domestic servants, calling the San 'savages' even while their lives epitomised gentleness in contrast to the whites' brutality. Of all the novels which discuss racial prejudice and the nature of institutionalised apartheid, only *The Sound of the Gora* explores the historical role of religion in the justification of apartheid. The Boer paterfamilias at evening prayers reads and preaches on the Biblical curse on Canaan, arguing on religious grounds that the Afrikaners are a chosen race. Still preaching in religious terms, he deplores the refusal of the San to adopt the capitalist values of 'owning your own piece of land, of cultivating your crops, of herding your cattle' (68). Although the 1800 plot of this novel resembles that of Seed's *The New Fire*, Harries goes further in suggesting complexity. Like Seed, she uses the San point of view to good effect – for example, a child is caught by an 'evil-smelling Boer' (18) – but the ways of the Boers are also studied, such as the paradoxical behaviour of the woman who lovingly clothes the little San girl in antique velvet.

How black people are portrayed

Most of the novels that deal with race relations in modern times do not employ black protagonists to give an Afrocentric perspective. The central characters are white, and the books are clearly intended for white readers who will identify with them. The writers use this identification to let the readers experience what will be, for most of them, new modes of relationships with black people, to see black people in what may be a new light and to listen, with the characters, to what blacks say they think and feel. In the young adult fiction particularly, the readers can share with the protagonist a growth in understanding and development in relations between black and white.

A typical relationship is that between a white child and the child of a domestic servant or farm employee. One's immediate reaction might be to say that this is a traditional relationship in South Africa, approved of and even sentimentalised in white society, especially on farms. In *A Cageful of Butterflies* by Lesley Beake, the position is formalised when Mponyane is brought from his hut to become Frank's *umtalaan*, his 'closest person' (2), though already there is a difference in that he is treated as one of the white family. Where these books really depart from the traditional representation is that the friendship continues into teenagehood – even to the point where innocent friendship turns to dawning adolescent love (in *Streams to Rivers*). What is more, the black children are proud, intelligent, educated, articulate and speak English fluently.

In their efforts to suggest that such friendships can be normal, the writers perhaps exceed the bounds of probability for all but a very few people in contemporary South Africa. For example, the relatives of thirteen-year-old Kate of *Witch Woman on the Hogsback* allow her to go camping overnight with Luvuyo, their maid's son. Only occasionally are mutterings of disapproval heard: in *Borderline*, the white children sense that the woman house-sitting with them in the absence of their parents disapproves of their allowing Sipu, son of the farm foreman, into the house. Liz thinks, 'It was no good telling Mrs Bessell that Sipu was just like a brother and they all came into her room' (51), and her brother Jan innocently decides that the Bessells must be 'snobs'. Little does Mrs Bessell know that Liz is hiding a fifteen-year-old black stranger, a suspected terrorist, under her bed to shield him from the police.

Equally exceptional must be the ability of these black youths to speak fluent colloquial English. Some of the writers fudge this, and one is not quite sure whether the children are not perhaps speaking Xhosa, Sotho or Zulu; but young readers would probably not notice. In *Where the Marula Grows* by Grace Meyer, however, the question of language is addressed: we are told that Themba's English is improving – though he often exclaims in Sotho – and that although his white friend Peter speaks Northern Sotho fluently they prefer to speak English together. Their friend Ben Venter is never labelled an Afrikaner, but he in turn makes exclamations such as 'Jislaaik' and 'Ag foeitog'. Peter's mother calmly reflects, 'How fortunate the twins were to have such good friends close by' (10).

All in all the effect is that the reader experiences young black people as quite ordinary, though they may be interesting and

135

different. A little touch of narrative technique which contributes to this ordinariness is the dropping of racial epithets. When Thesen wrote *A Deadly Presence*, everyone was labelled, for example as a 'coloured labourer', whether it was germane or not; but in most recent novels (of which Kenmuir's *The Tusks and the Talisman* is a good example) one can only distinguish people's race from their names or incidental clues. This effect of ordinariness is central to many books; even though the plots are a little far-fetched for the present, they enable the authors to anticipate a new dispensation in South Africa and encourage their readers to explore new modes of living that it will make possible.

Just as friendships between black and white children were traditionally approved in white South African society since they were no threat to the social structure, so too the relationship between whites and family servants has had a sentimental place in white lore. The novels which introduce liberated young black people still include their mothers as domestic servants who are portrayed as loving dispensers of food and comfort. To Michelle of *Streams to Rivers*, Pauline is a surrogate mother, always smelling of soap. Caroline, in *The Sound of the Gora*, parallels Michelle exactly, for she too is motherless and turns to their domestic servant, writing in her diary, 'I don't get close to people. Except Dora, of course. But then she's like a mother. I don't even notice she's black' (117). These two books are largely perpetuating the traditional relationship, just as Jenny Seed does in *The Spy Hill*, with its theme of the 'faithful retainer', of master and servant ready to lay down their lives for each other. But this theme was brilliantly turned upside down as long ago as 1947 by Herman Charles Bosman in his short story 'Makapan's Caves', and some youth novels also look at it in a new light.

Go well, Stay well analyses at length the implications of employing domestic servants – 'the nameless ones'. Typically, Candy, teenage girl from a wealthy home, reflects, 'The only black men she had come across were servants in white households, and their servility had stamped them with an almost sexless identity in her mind' (20). Paul Geraghty's autobiographical novel *Pig* gives a new twist to a boy's relationship with an old man by relating how Mike, a desperately unhappy white boy from Natal where he had a Zulu *umtalaan*, seeks the friendship of the Xhosa groundsman at his new school in Cape Town, in order to gain solace and advice on how to handle his bullying, racist schoolmates. In that intolerant environment their friendship is defiant and has to be kept secret. Another stereotype is avoided when Mike sees the old man drunk. There is none of the amusing, foolish *outa* about him, and Mike simply feels embarrassment.

Across some two dozen novels on contemporary themes it is possible to detect a pattern in the way black people are presented. In the books where all the characters are black, there are some bad people and some who, by force of circumstance, have turned criminal or been brutalised, but in general black people are portrayed as good, caring, warm and loving. This can be seen in four novels depicting harsh urban life, three of them being about 'coloured' people – *The Sound of the Gora* about Woodstock, *Love, David* by Dianne Case about the Cape Flats, and *The Strollers* by Lesley Beake, winner of the 1988 Percy FitzPatrick Award, about street children and 'Bergies' in Cape Town. Another book about street children, this time in Johannesburg, is the poorly written *Out of the Twilight* by Phyllis Owen. Although the stories contain graphic and at times disturbing incidents, these are ameliorated by the mutual support that the children give each other, and golden-hearted whores and wine-drinking, card-playing lotus-eaters whom they encounter.

So far I have indicated that the apparent realism of these novels is actually a deliberately slanted portrayal. Realism turns even more to romanticism when, often, it is *rural* black people who are shown to be the most welcoming and tolerant. An intriguing dimension is added to this by a theme which appears in three novels. In *A Cageful of Butterflies*, when little Frank flees to his companion Mponyane's kraal as the only escape he can think of from the bullying he is subjected to at school, he is unwittingly repeating his mother's act when at the age of eighteen she went to live with rural black people. Similarly, Michelle of *Streams to Rivers* wants to live with blacks in the country, encouraged in this idea by Pauline and the thought of her friend, Pauline's grandson, going to the hills for initiation. Only later does Michelle learn from her father that she had unwittingly wished to repeat history, for her late mother had wanted to take her to live with black friends in Swaziland – 'so that you wouldn't grow up believing that you were better than them, or that they were different to you' (24). *Go well, Stay well* ends with the pair of friends, one black

137

and one white, overcoming resistance from the white girl's parents to go on holiday together to stay with the black girl's rural relatives in Swaziland, where their relationship can be normal.

In these identical incidents we have, perhaps, a new literary legend to add to those others that are well known in South African literature and which crop up again in youth novels – Jim-comes-to-Jo'burg *(Out of the Twilight)*, and Try-for-white *(The Sound of the Gora)*. The romanticism of this legend of whites going to live with blacks in the country is shown up by contrasting it with the negative version in Nadine Gordimer's *July's People*, which describes a black rural community acting as unwilling hosts to white refugees.

'Michelle's mom had been a woman of the land' (16): frequently the stories have characters remarking that the land is beautiful. Country people, both black and white, are portrayed as caring and healing, whereas city people are hypocrites and bigots, often leading lives of personal immorality. Michelle's liberal friends react to the city by furnishing their house with natural and hand-crafted articles – it has a 'feel of Africa' (55). The stereotype – which is presented uncritically by the author – is reinforced by the remark of her cousin that they 'burn incense and eat herbs and things' (44). Another example is the rescue of the children in *Borderline* in what may be Swaziland or Mocambique. They are met by members of the newly victorious government in exile, including Alizene, an idealised black woman – 'a tall woman in a long cotton skirt', speaking a strange language – who soothes Liz's skin with an unguent made of herbs picked in the bush. Liz is dressed by her in a similar skirt and around her neck a cabinet minister hangs an antique ivory necklace. The children are taken to a table under the trees,

> laid with woven reed mats and wooden bowls full of fruit; orange-coloured pawpaws, round and juicy watermelon cut in slices and a huge gourd of maas, the soured milk that Thandi made for them sometimes. Liz spooned the creamy mealie-meal porridge into her wooden bowl and covered it with brown sauce ... They munched their way through the sweet flesh of the pawpaws and melons, spitting out the soft pips. (110)

138

This repast of natural foods, served by a Mother Africa figure, affirms the goodness of the land and its people.

A novel by a black writer about rural people gives a different picture. Es'kia Mphahlele's *Father Come Home* is a strongly didactic children's story extolling the organic unity of the tribe, the importance of its traditions, respect for the ancestors, and the moral values which children should learn. In its very style it resembles oral tradition: it is a rambling, episodic tale, with many digressions recounting history and customs and quoting praise poems. Yet although the story goes back to 1913, it recounts no rural idyll, for the practice of migrant labour and the personal tragedies of accidents on the mines impinge heavily on the villagers. The novel concludes with the central character, now an old man, meeting a childhood friend and narrating how he has led what was, on the whole, a good and satisfying life. Together they affirm the values of their early upbringing and the part played by relatives and neighbours.

Another children's book with a black protagonist, also by a black writer, is *A Message in the Wind* by Chris van Wyk, which links tribal history with modern city life. Two modern boys from rival tribes go back in a time-machine to seek the origin of the feud which has persisted even in the city. A feeble, amateurish little story, it spells out its moral at the end, when both boys hear 'a voice in the wind .... It said that men must forget their differences and live together, in love, in peace' (66).

Many of these novels, as the examples which I have quoted show, have a sense of history repeating itself, or at any rate of the past living in the present. *A Message in the Wind* expresses through the device of time-travel a wish to go back and change the past in order to make the present better. However, it is not only the divisions, but also the healings, of the past that can be repeated in the present. In *The Sound of the Gora*, the music of the gora, which brought together the lonely little San girl and the son of her white master, also brings together two modern children, white Caroline and coloured Andre, and it unites Caroline with her sister. After discovering that her late mother had been classified coloured but had successfully lived as a white, Caroline leaves her loveless home to live with the sister who had been brought up among coloured people. As Andre's father teaches them, 'Mantis brings together things that have come apart' (92).

When even a new cycle of history cannot heal wrongs, there can still be hope. Before he dies, the conservationist of *Kobie and the Military Road* teaches Kobie, 'Out of this suffering will come strength that you never had before' (55); the old Xhosa groundsman in *Pig* leaves the white boy equipped to fight his own battles. San belief in a new life after death can sustain hope. Ann Harries, author of *The Sound of the Gora*, draws on the same San sources as Marguerite Poland to express this hope of regeneration, such as when the little San girl prays to the moon,

> *Once when your child the hare*
> *cried to you, his mother, not to let him die*
> *you told us too that when we died*
> *we should return again. (77)*[2]

That Harries should use ancient San beliefs to effect reconciliation, not only through historical flashback but also through fantasy, is significant. Andreé-Jeanne Tötemeyer has pointed out in a seminal article that the key youth literature texts in reconciling black and white in South Africa are the fantasies in which white children join forces with the power of indigenous myth to overcome evil: *Witch Woman on the Hogsback* by Carolyn Parker and *The Battle of the Mountain* by Judy Chalmers, which were discussed in Chapter Four, and *The Sound of the Gora*.[3] In *Witch Woman* the white girl, Kate, is singled out by the People of the River, *a Bantu bamlambo*, as having the power to overcome a white witch from the North who has invaded their land – she believes in northern witches as well as Xhosa spirits. In *The Battle of the Mountain* Pippa joins forces against the evil Igwain with San people who live in caves inside the mountain and who recognise her as specially blessed. We can recall, too, the respect that Rosie of Poland's *Shadow of the Wild Hare* shows for Xhosa beliefs. These novels show that reconciliation of black and white must take place on a spiritual plane as well as through intellectual understanding and forgiveness of the past.

Apart from these sincere attempts to bring cultures together through myth, references to traditional healers, the throwing of the bones, and tokoloshes appear in many youth novels. In *Where the Marula Grows* an unexplained incident in which the children find a set of *ditaola* or *dolosse*, which frightens Themba, is an opportu-

140

nity for his mother to explain, 'We're Christians. The two just don't go together. Black magic has caused so much unnecessary suffering to our people' (29). Although the *nyanga* whose bones give the title to *Dry Bones Rattling* turns out to be a fraud, his performance is dramatic enough:

> *The hideous creature ceased its gyrating and lay face down in the dirt, a ragged heap of filthy skins and oily fish bladders, fingers and toes twitching convulsively. Then it moved, rising like a malignant black molehill from the earth, hissing like a monitor lizard ... The loathsome mound moved up, growing like a black toadstool, repulsive and stinking. (51)*

No wonder Kenmuir added a mollifying author's note to the effect that 'Nyangas are also very real, but fortunately they are usually respectable people, plying an honest trade'. Even the co-driver of the pantechnikon in which Kobie hitches a ride to Cape Town (in *Kobie and the Military Road*) turns out to be a dab hand at the bones, though after he has dressed up in his regalia light relief is added when he admonishes Kobie, 'Get the dawg outa here. If she pees on the bones the ancient spirits gonna freak out' (102).

It seems that for all too many white writers, black culture is still synonymous with witchdoctors and tokoloshes. Mphahlele, it is true, also includes an incident in *Father Come Home* when the villagers ask old Mashabela to prophesy, but, significantly, he cannot give an answer. As I pointed out in Chapter Four, whites like to believe that Africa is mysterious. Grace Meyer, in *Where the Marula Grows*, even makes a mockery of the Stone Age with a ridiculous account of a cave with a secret pivoted door, in which stone artefacts with 'inscriptions' on them are discovered arranged on ledges. Dr Nthato Motlana gave his verdict on whites' fixation on witchdoctors in an interview published in *The Weekly Mail* in 1991:

> *Dr Nthato Motlana, a medical practioner and Soweto community leader, said sangomas were 'charlatans' who fooled people with the 'superstitious mumbo-jumbo' which they claimed was science. Motlana lamented that whites 'romanticised' sangomas. 'They invite them to conferences*

> *where the sangomas talk s..t. And the Europeans write it
> up as our culture. Black culture is not rubbish.'*[4]

By insisting on blacks' 'superstition', white writers maintain the 'otherness' and 'primitiveness' of black people.

Even when white writers for children are not romanticising, it is not easy for them to portray black characters authentically or create a plot that will convincingly engage them with white people. It is as though these writers are, in this respect, at the stage that William Plomer was at when he wrote *Turbott Wolfe* in 1925, compensating for a lack of first-hand knowledge and literary models by creating melodramatic plots and characters, yet at the same time breaking new ground in bringing black people in as *people*. All too easily, the black characters are marginalised. Two years after Andreé-Jeanne Tötemeyer pointed out, at the national symposium on children's literature in South Africa held in 1987, that 'black characters play subordinate roles ... They talk less and often die tragically – their white counterparts usually recover,'[5] Lesley Beake published *A Cageful of Butterflies,* in which the deaf-mute Mponyane drowns while saving his *umtalaan* Frank. The novel gained Beake her second Percy FitzPatrick Award, making her and Marguerite Poland at that time the only two recipients of the prize, both of them also having won it twice. To do her justice, she does say in an author's note, 'Mponyane was real. He lived and died in Northern Natal fifteen years ago. He couldn't hear and he couldn't speak, but he gave.'

Another way in which blacks are subordinated is by depicting them as helpless victims. In *A Sudden Summer*, for example, although the homeless coloured girl proudly resists the attempts of the white girl to help her family, unexpected events allow the whites to intervene and play Father Christmas in finding them a home and a job for the father.

Perhaps it can be argued that, at least in the novels with an astutely observant white narrator, such as Bransby's *Homeward Bound* (written as a teenager's diary) and Bregin's *The Kayaboeties*, the marginalised position of blacks is brought home, but even then Jay Heale is justified in commenting on the latter, 'We have yet to see a book about one white boy being allowed into a black gang ...'[6] Regardless of the merits of individual books, they still fit into the pattern that Tötemeyer has identified.

The endings of the novels can also be seen in two ways. To take a few examples: the incipient romance between the white girl and the black boy in *Streams to Rivers* is put on hold when he leaves for an 'international school in Swaziland', where she hopes to join him later; the friendship between the white girl and the black girl in *Go well, Stay well*, confined to the claustrophobic bedroom where they meet, will be able to flourish when they leave for their holiday in Swaziland; the young black 'terrorist' of *Borderline* takes his rightful place across the border. In *Homeward Bound*, the only black boy in the white school returns to the township at mid-year after threats to his father for being a 'sell-out', but not before he has changed the lives of many at the school. Are these deaths or escapes to non-racial countries, or disappearances from the lives of the whites, a cop-out by the authors, or the only realistic way they can end with a message of hope?

Racism and its ramifications

The marginalised position of blacks is not always something that readers have to infer from the pattern of the plots in modern youth novels: a number of them make social issues and the nature of racism their focus. A pioneering effort was *Go well, Stay well*, published in 1979. By comparison with the angry books of a decade later, it reads as too bland and bent upon being informative – the reader is never taken into Soweto with Becky, the black girl, but learns about everything, including her rape, through what she tells her white friend. By far the angriest, most heartfelt explorations of racism are the two outstanding youth novels, *Down Street* (1989) and *Homeward Bound* (1990) by Lawrence Bransby, a young teacher at Ixopo High School. Both are narrated by white youths, thus conveying with immediacy the raw impressions and emotions of naive, ill-educated schoolboys who are forced to examine for the first time the nature of racism in South Africa and their own response to it. *Down Street* is the best – and also the most devastating – South African youth novel on this theme that I have read. Ted, the narrator, is a boarder at a country school who meets and falls in love with a waitress at a coffee bar, only to discover later that she is a 'coloured'. His parents, teachers, schoolmates and the local townspeople are shocked; her parents tell him it is best that they part and he ends up being assaulted by coloured youths for messing with one of their girls, and thrashed by his headmaster.

Homeward Bound is the diary of Jason, a Std 10 boarder at what would appear to be the same school, in which he describes the events of his final year, including the arrival of a sole black matric pupil. This book is even more shocking in its portrayal of crude racism, in that it records the white narrator's own initial racist reaction and the behaviour of his classmates – so much so that Jason (Bransby?) prefaces the diary with a warning to the reader that, though he has changed since then, 'It's rough. It's unpleasant, but that's how it was' (6).

Bransby's novels, written as they are by an insider, are an appalling indictment of white English-speaking society: the phoney, selfish, wife-swopping city parents who send their children out of the way to boarding school, the respectable bigotry of the country-folk, the cant of the teachers and the gross, bestial behaviour of the youthful male products of this society. His books are an indictment of the educational system and its values, which permeate many aspects of South African society. Racism forms part of a cluster of attitudes and behaviour endemic in the microcosm of the school, also to be found among the cruel, bullying, racist primary school boys of Cape Town portrayed by another young Natalian, Paul Geraghty, in *Pig*, and the children of the school in Northern Natal, some of them also misfits from the city, in *A Cageful of Butterflies*. The arrogance of the young white Natalians in *Homeward Bound* governs their attitude towards everybody. It takes the black boy in the school, Sol, to reprimand them for their jingoistic prejudice towards Afrikaners, which he points out is simply another manifestation of racism.

Violence is part of the culture of the school: in the bullying and fighting among the boys, the canings by teachers, and the paramountcy of rugby. In *Homeward Bound* the First XV rugby coach encourages the team to drink illicit beers, and he incites them to cheat, use dirty play and work themselves up before a match by hitting their heads against the wall. When Jason objects, the coach scorns him as a 'secret poofter'. (After the captain eventually complains to the headmaster, the man is removed from the team but not the school.) Hardly surprisingly, the coach's name is Allcock – a Freudian name (did Bransby realise this?) that symbolises the identification of masculinity with violence in this society. (In the

1960s there used to be a phallic competition among some boys'
high schools in Natal to have the tallest rugby goalposts on their
fields.)

Sexuality in the school takes a particular form. In *Homeward
Bound*, after inviting the girls to the spectacle, the matric boys line
up in the playground and expose their buttocks. A youth is ex-
pelled for his obscene baiting of a woman teacher in class. School
rules proliferate to regulate under what circumstances boys and
girls may meet and how close to each other they may come. Sol is
the only person among pupils and teachers who shows concern for
his junior fag, who is in deep personal trouble (the child later
attempts suicide). For his compassion, Sol is accused of homo-
sexuality by the other boys. These incidents are manifestations of
how sex is associated with male assertiveness, callousness, obscen-
ity, prurience and homophobia.

The bigoted sexual attitudes are naturally associated in turn
with racism. When Jason is rebuffed by a clean-living girl for
making advances that treated her like a sex object, he admits in his
diary that his insensitivity to her paralleled his earlier attitude towards blacks. Other books make the same point: the girl narrator
of *The Kayaboeties*, referring to the boys' treatment of the black
boy, says, 'See, I knew a little bit about how it felt to stand there
and have them talking back and forth about you as if you were
deaf or stupid' (27). A typical conjunction of sexism and the marginalisation of blacks is reported by a student in *Day of the Kugel*
who says that the Zulu he was taught in class was typified by the
phrase 'amanthombazana exhibeni – the girls are in the cooking
hut' (75). Women writers, notably Elana Bregin, Dianne Hofmeyr
and Janet Smith, make the gruff, inarticulate fathers of the households more racially prejudiced than the mothers, who often act as
mediators.

In this environment, the greatest crime a white schoolboy can
commit is when Ted dates a coloured girl in Bransby's *Down
Street*. Though their friendship is smashed, Ted has one final ri-
poste for the headmaster which damns the system: 'Why is what I
did such a *crime*? ... Was it the fact that I was in school uniform
or that she was a coloured, Sir?' (108)

After the powerful writing of *Down Street* it is hard to condone
yet another ending that, like Bregin's *Warrior of Wilderness*, ech-
oes the ending of *Lord of the Flies*. Golding, it will be recalled,

wrote, 'Ralph wept for the end of innocence, the darkness of man's heart, and the fall through the air of the true, wise friend called Piggy' (248). Bransby ends, 'And I wept for the loss of innocence, for the dirtying of something that had been so pure and lovely, and for my loneliness' (110).

Bransby sets against the negative values of South African society the positive power of Christianity. Although in *Down Street* a teacher is castigated for his hypocrisy in organising a multi-racial church function for pupils to 'Meet Your Brother' and then is disapproving of Ted's friendship with a coloured girl, in *Homeward Bound* it is the love of a Christian group in the school, headed by an exchange student (not a South African) that brings Jason friendship and inner peace.

The virulence of the racism in these two books, and its close identification with both the official and the hidden curricula of the schools, had an astonishing parallel in real life at the same time that *Homeward Bound* was published, when the case of the 'Frank Joubert Kaffir Bashing Society' was heard in the Grahamstown Supreme Court in 1991. Four former pupils of an English-medium white boys' high school in the Eastern Cape that is similar in situation and style to the schools in Bransby's novels (except that his are co-educational) were found guilty of culpable homicide and assault with intent to do grievous bodily harm after causing the death of an elderly vagrant by beating him with hockey sticks, a knuckleduster, a truncheon and a cricket wicket. They were members of a society in the school hostel which, apparently for years, had gone out at night to assault blacks.

At the trial, the headmaster was quoted as having told the school assembly that if boys found vagrants damaging school property they should take a 'two-by-four' plank to them, and the judge found that 'incidents of a similar nature at the school had been tolerated'. A similar incident in which white schoolboys were alleged to have killed a black vagrant occurred at an Afrikaans-medium school in Nelspruit, in the Transvaal Lowveld, about five years previously.

The Cape headmaster was quoted in the *Sunday Times* as saying in his evidence that the school's values

> *are those of an English public school ... Our values haven't altered in 130 years. I suppose we could sum them*

146

*up as honesty, decency and hard work, words that are go-
ing out of fashion perhaps.*[7]

It is revealing that he should call upon the ghosts of British imperialism in his school's defence, for, as I pointed out in Chapter
Three, the South African school system is descended from that of
the British public schools. The schools of Bransby's novels and the
'kaffir bashing societies' of the real-life Eastern Cape and Eastern
Transvaal are a harsh commentary on the combination of the heri-
tage of the nineteenth century public schools and twentieth century
Christian National Education to be found in South Africa today.

Bransby's frank exploration of a cluster of the more unseemly
values of an English-medium white school contrasts with the approach of a contemporary Afrikaans youth novel, *The Horizons of
the Hunter* (1987) by W.S. Sutherland, translated into English by
Beverley van Reenen, which also deals with manliness, race relations and attitudes towards women. A hunting adventure set at the
end of the Anglo-Boer War, it opens by announcing that 'any boy
worthy of his sex' (4) likes hunting. This is given as a truth universally acknowledged, not as an historically placed view. (In an
effort to give a new slant to hunting, the author includes a gro-
tesque adventure in which the boys fall in a game pit, missing the
stakes, only to be followed by a herd of wildebeest stampeded by
a veld fire. The boys escape by hacking their way upwards
through the carcasses.) The white boy, Otto, longs to enjoy a
'David-and-Jonathan' friendship with a black boy, Bishwa, similar
to his father's friendship with a chief, and Bishwa reciprocates by
hero-worshipping him for, as the chief says, blacks can learn from
whites:

> *That's typical of my people. When we are frightened, we
> drop everything and run. In war as well, if we have been
> beaten and the enemy has put us to flight, we throw down
> our weapons and flee. White people also run away, but
> they take their weapons with them, and may return to fight
> again. That's something we need to learn. (71)*

As for attitudes towards women, Otto adores his sister, saying to
himself, 'The man that got his sister would have to be one in a
thousand, a man that would not hurt her gentle spirit' (86). He

muses that he would like to marry a girl like her.

Sutherland probably thought he was being very modern and enlightened in writing this book, but it propagates without question values which are as much a part of the 'discourse of imperialism'[8] as those that Bransby attacks: the machismo of the Bushveld hunter; patronising of blacks who are safely set apart as being at a lower stage of development; and the placing of women on a pedestal, which was only another way in which women were marginalised in Victorian times.

Iconoclastic writing

Bransby's novels are typical of the best modern South African youth novels on social issues in the way they create immediacy through diction and style. The language is often what used to be considered coarse. We have Ted introducing his school in *Down Street*: 'I mean, anyone would think we were some pain-in-the-arse private school or something, the way they go on' (1); and the narrator of *Pig* talking about the school groundsman:

> *Somehow Johannes never seemed to give up, even though he had nothing going for himself. I mean, when you're sixty-five or whatever, and little white school kids still laugh and call you a coon boy, when the hell do you become a man? (72)*

The authentic slang and the zest of the writing reflect the youthfulness of many of the authors. Sometimes the child narrators get quite 'naughty': Charlie, the twelve-year-old girl who narrates *The Kayaboeties*, explains that one of the boys, whose mother calls him Dickie, is called Pecker by his friends as a double joke because 'he was always fiddling with himself, with – you know – "it" ' (2).

This flaunting of taboos easily turns to satire, which enlivens several books. Peter Younghusband's *Kobie and the Military Road* has leitmotivs of humour in it that are satirical as well as ameliorating the pathos. (Young Kobie was seriously injured in a landmine explosion in the Northern Transvaal that killed his parents.) One of these recurring jokes concerns the State President who wags his finger, but who meets his match in his wife:

> *'Don't you shake your finger at me, Papa! You can shake*
> *your finger at the Progressive Federal Party. You can*
> *shake your finger at the United Nations, and at Washing-*
> *ton and at London and at the ANC and at Chief Buthelezi.*
> *But you can't shake your finger at me!' What she said was*
> *perfectly true. He could not shake his finger at her. It was*
> *the best-kept secret in the government. (120)*

Another standing joke is that people are always asking Kobie if his dog will do 'you-know-what' on the floor; it never does, until it goes for a ride in the Presidential airplane. However, an Air Force officer assures him, 'Never mind. We'll attend to it. The Air Force can handle any crisis' (126).

Sacred cows are also demolished by the witty dialogue of Barbara Ludman's *Day of the Kugel*, such as when the American girl's South African friends sardonically teach her how to be a kugel: 'You love black babies and they love you ... As a kugel, your politics are based on people, not on issues ... You wish the government would stop hassling your maid' (8).

Humour has another role in *The Strollers*, a moving story which is nevertheless flawed by sentimentality, facetiousness and weaknesses in narrative technique. In addition to sly digs such as when the children are unsuccessful in begging at a house called 'Costa Plenty', it has a memorable comic character in the form of a foppish gangster. These touches provide comic relief from what is actually the appalling world of homeless children.

In engaging the young reader through the diction, the daring, the rage, the bewilderment, the *angst* of the adolescent characters, the best writers are inciting the readers to action. Difficult though it may be for young people to make a difference in the world, those in the novels *act*. The thoughts of Candy at the end of *Go well, Stay well* sum this up:

> *But she was afraid to be too optimistic. There was a long,*
> *long way to go yet, and she had a feeling that time was*
> *running out. All the same, she told herself, simply to have*
> *started was something; at least there was hope in that*
> *(202).*

Unlike Seed's historical characters, who were confined to personal

149

struggles, more emancipated modern times provide more scope for political action for young people. And so we find that, though the novels still have something of a liberal-humanist concern for 'interiority', they are also concerned with political processes. Richard Rive criticised the liberal literature pioneered by Alan Paton for being 'personalised, showing greater concern for the victim than with the acts of victimisation',[9] but these youth novelists have young people explore the historical aetiology of apartheid that lies in the Afrikaners' civil religion, British imperialism and capitalism, and the young people show concern for the processes of victimisation as well as the victims themselves.

In the novels the young people are ready for change while the adults are bogged down with caution, and similarly the fate of the novels themselves reflects this difference. The youthfulness and daring of the style and subject matter of these books speak to a youthful audience, which is no doubt why they make white adults uncomfortable. At least one of them (*The Sound of the Gora*) was banned for a while, and many of them do not appear in public libraries or on the approved lists of white education departments.

In one respect, though, the books may appear to be less modern than their adult counterparts. With only two exceptions they confine themselves to traditional, linear narrative modes, whereas postmodernism favours disruption of modes of representation in order to subvert conventional thinking – John Conyngham's *The Arrowing of the Cane* and the novels of André P. Brink and J.M. Coetzee being good examples.

The first exception is Lesley Beake, who must have impressed the judges of the Percy FitzPatrick Award with her technique in *A Cageful of Butterflies*: she uses a broken time sequence and a variety of voices, including narration by a white woman and exceptionally powerful passages which convey the thoughts of the young black deaf-mute. However, complaints by librarians that the book is 'confusing' remind us that children's literature has to work within more constraints than adult literature.

The second exception is *The Sound of the Gora*. When it skips from narrative to extracts from a diary this is simply, perhaps, a frank way of confronting the handling of a change in centre of consciousness which, as I have remarked, local authors on the whole cannot manage. However, this novel also operates within two time frames, the present and 200 years ago. The introduction

150

of an ambiguous figure of a Bushman living in a cave on Table Mountain who links past and present brings this book closer to fantasy, which is another way in which fiction can break free of the realistic mode.

Myth and fantasy were perhaps the only way until the 1970s for children's literature in South Africa to subvert the reality of racial and cultural divide in the country. The imaginative and spiritual world of the San, Khoekhoen, African and Malay peoples could be entered by white children long before the physical barriers between them could be bridged. In the 1990s, children are still being enticed through books of folktales and fantasy to find, in the words of the San prayer, the 'sweet roots and honey' of myth and custom, but they are also being challenged by realist plots that reach to the bounds of credulity to explore the possibilities of a new society in South Africa and a new relationship between the people and their natural environment.

NOTES

1. Margaret Lenta, 'Black and white women yesterday and today,' *Current Writing*, 3, October 1991, 165.
2. Both Marguerite Poland and Ann Harries use the versions of San poems in *The Penguin Book of South African Verse*, ed. Jack Cope and Uys Krige, Harmondsworth: Penguin, 1968, but Harries does not acknowledge her source.
3. Andreé-Jeanne Tötemeyer, 'Impact of African mythology on South African juvenile literature,' *South African Journal of Library and Information Science*, 57:4, December 1989, 397.
4. Tshokolo wa Molakeng, 'Sangomas who won't give up an ancient power,' *Weekly Mail*, 18 February 1991, 22.
5. Andreé-Jeanne Tötemeyer, 'Towards interracial understanding through South African children's and youth literature,' in *Towards Understanding/Op Weg na Begrip*, ed. Isabel Cilliers, Cape Town: Maskew Miller Longman, 1988, 80.
6. Jay Heale, Review of *The Kayaboeties*, *Bookchat*, 92, January 1990, 23.
7. Reports in *The Star*, 16 February 1991, 2, and 6 March 1991, 2, and *The Sunday Times*, 17 February 1991, 5.
8. Dorothy Driver, ' "Woman" as sign in the South African colonial

enterprise,' *Journal of Literary Studies*, 4:1, March 1988, 13.
9. Richard Rive, 'The black writer and South African literature,' in *Towards Understanding/Op Weg na Begrip*, 203.

Bibliography

Adams, Richard. *Watership Down*. Harmondsworth: Puffin, 1973. First published, 1972.

Adey, David; Beeton, Ridley; Chapman, Michael and Pereira, Ernest. *Companion to South African English Literature*. Johannesburg: Ad Donker, 1986.

Anderson, W. and Groff, P. *A New Look at Children's Literature*. Belmont: Wadsworth, 1972.

Aristotle. *On the Art of Poetry*, trans. Ingram Bywater. Oxford: The Clarendon Press, 1920.

Barrie, J.M. *Peter and Wendy*. 1911.

Baumann, K. *Puss in Boots. Based on the Classic Tale by Charles Perrault*. London: Abelard/North South, 1982.

Baumbach, E.J.M. and Marivate, C.T.D. *Xironga Folk-tales*. Pretoria: University of South Africa, 1973.

Beake, Lesley. *A Cageful of Butterflies*. Cape Town: Maskew Miller Longman, 1989.

Beake, Lesley. *The Strollers*. Cape Town: Maskew Miller Longman, 1987.

Bedford, Emma. 'Illustrated children's books in South Africa,' in *Doerland-y/Far far away: South African Illustrated Children's Books*, ed. Marianne Hölscher. Cape Town: South African National Gallery, 1986, 20-27.

Bezant, N.G. *Everlasting Footprints and Other Strange Stories of South African People*. Cape Town: Central News Agency, 1953.

Bleek, D.F. 'Special speech of animals and moon used by the /Xam bushmen.' *Bantu Studies*, X, 1936, 163-199.

Bleek, D.F. *The Mantis and His Friends: Bushman Folklore*. Collected

153

by the late Dr W.H.I. Bleek and the late Dr Lucy C. Lloyd. Cape Town: Masker Miller, 1923.

Bleek, W.H.I. 'Remarks on "A glimpse into the mythology of the Maluti Bushmen," by J.M. Orpen'. *The Cape Monthly Magazine*, IX: 49, July 1874, 1-13.

Bleek, W.H.I. *Reynard the Fox in South Africa, or Hottentot Fables and Tales*. London: Trubner & Co., 1864.

Blount, Margaret. *Animal Land: The Creatures of Children's Fiction*. London: Hutchinson, 1974.

Bobbins, G.M.H. *The Twilight of English*. Cape Town: Maskew Miller, 1951.

Bond, John. *They Were South Africans*. Cape Town: Oxford University Press, 1956.

Bond, Michael. *A Bear called Paddington*. London: Collins, 1970.

Bosman, Herman Charles. 'Makapan's Caves', in *Mafeking Road*. Cape Town: Human & Rousseau, 1969. First published 1947.

Boswell, J. *The Life of Samuel Johnson*. 3 vols. London: Swan Sonnenschein, Lowrey & Co., 1888.

Bowes-Taylor, Gorry. 'The mouse grows whiskers.' *The Argus*, 22 September 1983, 15.

Branford, Jean. *A Dictionary of South African English*. Cape Town: Oxford University Press, 1978.

Branford, William. 'A Dictionary of South African English as a reflex of the English-speaking cultures of South Africa,' in *English-speaking South Africa Today*, ed. André de Villiers. Oxford: Oxford University Press, 1976, 297-316.

Bransby, Lawrence. *Down Street*. Cape Town: Tafelberg, 1989.

Bransby, Lawrence. *Homeward Bound*. Cape Town: Tafelberg, 1990.

Bregin, Elana. *The Kayaboeties*. Cape Town: Maskew Miller Longman, 1989.

Bregin, Elana. *Warrior of Wilderness*. Cape Town: Maskew Miller Longman, 1989.

Brown, Vivienne Johns. *The Boy and the Tree*. Illus. Elizabeth Andrew. Cape Town: Human & Rousseau, 1989.

Brownlee, Frank. *Cattle Thief: The Story of Ntsukumbini*. London: Cape, 1960. First published 1929.

Buchan, John. *Prester John*. First published 1910.

Bulpin, T.V. *The Hunter is Death*. Johannesburg: Nelson, 1962.

Burnet, Frances Hodgson. *The Secret Garden*. 1911.

Butler, Guy. *Take Root or Die*. Cape Town: Balkema, 1970.

Butler, Guy, ed. *When Boys Were Men*. Cape Town: Oxford University Press, 1969.

Callaway, Henry. *Nursery Tales, Traditions and Histories of the Zulus, in their Own Words, with a Translation into English, and Notes*. Vol. 1. Springvale, Natal: J.A. Blair, 1868.

Cartwright, A.P. *The First South African: The Life and Times of Sir Percy FitzPatrick*. Cape Town: Purnell, 1971.

Case, Diane. *Love, David*. Cape Town: Maskew Miller Longman, 1986.

Chalmers, Judy. *The Battle of the Mountain*. Cape Town: Human & Rousseau, 1984.

Chapman, Michael.'A sense of identity.' *CRUX*, 24:1, February 1990, 34-45.

Chaucer, Geoffrey. *The Nonne Preestes Tale*, in *The Complete Works of Geoffrey Chaucer*, ed. W.W. Skeat. Oxford: Oxford University Press, 1912, 543-550.

Chilvers, Hedley. *The Seven Lost Trails of Africa*. London: Cassell, 1930.

Clacherty, A.J. 'Towards an environmental education programme for the training of primary school teachers.' Unpublished MSc dissertation. Cape Town: University of Cape Town, 1988.

Coetzee, J.M. *Dusklands*. Johannesburg: Ravan, 1974.

Coetzee, J.M. *In the Heart of the Country*. London: Secker & Warburg, 1977.

Coetzer, J.P., ed. *Tales of Veld and Vlei*. Cape Town: Maskew Miller, 1964.

Conyngham, John. *The Arrowing of the Cane*. Johannesburg: Ad Donker, 1986.

Cope, Jack. *Tales of the Trickster Boy*. Cape Town: Tafelberg, 1990.

Cope, Jack and Krige, Uys (eds). *The Penguin Book of South African Verse*. Harmondsworth: Penguin, 1968.

Davis, F. *Yearning for Yesterday: a Sociology of Nostalgia*. New York: The Free Press, 1979.

De Klerk, Vivian. 'An investigation into the language of English-speaking adolescents, with particular reference to sex, age and type of school.' Unpublished PhD thesis. Cape Town: University of Cape Town, 1989.

De Villiers, R.M., ed. *Better Than They Knew*. 2 vols. Cape Town: Purnell, 1972 and 1974.

Dickens, Charles. *Hard Times*. 1862.

Driver, Dorothy. ' "Woman" as sign in the South African colonial enterprise.' *Journal of Literary Studies*, 4:1, March 1988, 3-20.

Du Plessis, I.D. *Uit die Slamse Buurt: Kaapse Sprokies, Fabels en Legendes*. Cape Town: Nasionale Pers, 1939.

Du Preez, Hanneke. *Kgalagadi Tales: Bushman One*. Alberton: Librarius Felicitas, 1984.

Du Preez, Hanneke. *Kgalagadi Tales: Bushman Two*. Alberton: Librarius

Felicitas, 1985.

Dymond, Ann. *Borderline*. Pretoria: Daan Retief, 1986.

Elliot, Geraldine. *The Long Grass Whispers*. London: Routledge & Kegan Paul, 1939.

Fairbridge, Kingsley. *The Story of Kingsley Fairbridge by Himself*. London and Cape Town: Oxford University Press, 1958. First published as *The Autobiography of Kingsley Fairbridge*, 1927.

Fairlady. 'African fantasy.' January 1984, 11.

Farrar, F.W. *Eric, or Little by Little*. Edinburgh: Adam & Charles Black, 1858. Facsimile reprint by Garland Publishing Inc., New York and London, 1976.

Finnegan, Ruth. *Oral Literature in Africa*. Oxford: Oxford University Press, 1970.

FitzPatrick, Percy. *Jock of the Bushveld*. London: Longmans, Green & Co., 1907.

Flemming, Leonard. *A Fool on the Veld*. Cape Town: Argus, 1916.

Flemming, Leonard. *The Call of the Veld*. Bloemfontein: White, 1924.

Gallagher, Joan. 'The creator of animal fairy-tales – Marguerite Poland.' *Artes Natales*, April 1983, 8-10.

Geraghty, Paul. *Pig*. Cape Town: Maskew Miller Longman, 1989.

Gertz, Bon. 'Jenny Seed interviewed.' *The Cape Librarian*, March 1979, 2-8.

Golding, William. *Lord of the Flies*. London: Faber & Faber, 1962. First published 1954.

Goldstuck, Arthur. *The Rabbit in the Thorn Tree: Modern Myths and Urban Legends of South Africa*. Harmondsworth: Penguin, 1990.

Gordimer, Nadine. *A World of Strangers*. London: Victor Gollancz, 1958.

Gordimer, Nadine. *July's People*. Johannesburg: Ravan Press, 1981.

Gordimer, Nadine. *The Lying Days*. London: Victor Gollancz, 1953.

Grahame, Kenneth. *The Golden Age*. 1895.

Grahame, Kenneth. *The Wind in the Willows*. London: Methuen, 1981. First published, 1908.

Gray, Stephen. 'A working position,' in *Momentum: On Recent South African Writing*, ed. M.J. Daymond, J.U. Jacobs and M. Lenta. Pietermaritzburg: University of Natal Press, 1984, 35-36.

Gray, Stephen. 'Domesticating the wilds: J. Percy FitzPatrick's *Jock of the Bushveld* as a historical record for children.' *English in Africa*, 14:2, October 1987, 1-14.

Gray, Stephen. *Southern African Literature: An Introduction*. Cape Town: David Philip, 1979.

Greaves, Nick. *When Hippo was Hairy and Other Tales from Africa*. Manzini and Durban: Bok Books, 1988.

Green, Lawrence. *Great African Mysteries*. London: Paul, 1937.

Green, Lawrence. *Old Africa's Last Secrets*. London: Putnam, 1961.

Green, Lawrence. *Strange Africa*. London: Paul, 1938.

Green, Lawrence. *There's a Secret Hid Away*. Cape Town: Howard Timmins, 1956.

Grobbelaar, Pieter W. *The Earth must be Free*. Illus. Alida Bothma. Pretoria: Daan Retief, 1984.

Grobler, Hilda. 'Me Tarzan - you Jane: sex stereotyping in children's books,' in *Towards Understanding/Op Weg Na Begrip*, ed. Isabel Cilliers. Cape Town: Maskew Miller Longman, 1988, 126-141.

Haarhoff, Dorian. *The Wild South-West: Frontier Myths and Metaphors in Literature set in Namibia, 1760-1988*. Johannesburg: Witwatersrand University Press, 1991.

Haresnape, Geoffrey, ed. *The Great Hunters*. Cape Town: Purnell, 1974.

Harries, Ann. *The Sound of the Gora*. London: Heinemann Educational Books, 1984. First published 1980.

Heale, Jay. 'South African children's books in English,' in *Doer-Land-y/Far Far Away*, ed. Marianne Hölscher. Cape Town: South African National Gallery, 1980, 11-15.

Heale, Jay. 'Response to Nancy Schmidt.' *Newsletter of the United States Board on Books for Young People*, Fall 1986, 9.

Heale, Jay. 'Review of *The Kayaboeties*,' *Bookchat*, 92, January 1990, 23.

Heale, Jay. 'South African books.' *Bookchat*, 94, May 1990, 27.

Helfman, Elizabeth. *The Bushmen and their Stories*. New York: Seabury Press, 1971.

Henderson, May. *Looma, Teller of Tales: More Stories of Kruger Park*. Durban: Knox, 1943.

Henderson, May. *Mrs Mouse of Kruger Park*. Durban: Knox, 1944.

Henderson, May. *The Cock-Olly Book: Tales of Veld, Fun and Frolic*. Durban: Knox, 1941.

Henderson, May. *Tortoo the Tortoise: Ruler of Kruger Park*. Durban: Knox, 1943.

Hertslet, Jessie. *Bantu Folk Tales*. Cape Town: African Bookman, 1946.

Hickey, W.A. *Manela and the Poachers*. Pretoria: De Jager-HAUM, 1979.

Hickey, W.A. *Manela, the Bull Elephant: A Story for the Young at Heart*. Cape Town and Pretoria: De Jager-HAUM, 1976.

Hoban, Russell. *The Mouse and His Child*. Harmondsworth: Puffin, 1976. First published, 1967.

Hofmeyr, Dianne. *A Sudden Summer*. Cape Town: Tafelberg, 1987.

Hofmeyr, Dianne. *When Whales go Free*. Cape Town: Tafelberg, 1988.

Holland, Irma. *A Bushveld Story*. Johannesburg: Book Studio, 1987.

Honey, J.R. de S. 'Arnolds of the bushveld.' *Symposium*, 1975/76, 22-25.

Hughes, Thomas. *Tom Brown's School Days*. 1857.

Hunt, Peter. 'Arthur Ransome's *Swallows and Amazons*: escape to a lost paradise,' in *Touchstones: Reflections on the Best in Children's Literature*, ed. Perry Nodelman. West Lafayette: Children's Literature Association, 1985, 221-232.

Huntley, Brian. 'Rotating the cube,' in *Rotating the Cube: Environmental Strategies for the 1990s*, ed. Graham Howe. Durban: Department of Geographical and Environmental Sciences and Indicator Project South Africa, University of Natal, 1990, 111-115.

Jefferies, Richard. *Bevis*. 1877.

Jellicoe, Geoffrey and Susan. *The Landscape of Man: Shaping the Environment from Prehistory to the Present Day*. Revised second edition. London: Thames & Hudson, 1987.

Jenkins, Elwyn. 'Our teenagers are romantics.' *Transvaal Educational News*, 78:7, August 1981, 15-17.

Jenkins, Elwyn. 'The bushveld syndrome in South African English teaching.' *CRUX*, 11:4, October 1977, 17-22.

Jenkins, Elwyn. 'The nature of English Higher as a secondary school subject in the Transvaal, 1942-1972.' Unpublished MEd dissertation. Johannesburg: University of the Witwatersrand, 1973.

Joelson, Annette. *How the Ostrich got his Name and Other South African Stories for Children*. Cape Town: Juta, 1926.

Jones, Toeckey. *Go well, Stay well*. London: Bodley Head, 1979.

Joubert, Elsa. *The Four Friends and Other Tales from Africa*. Cape Town: Tafelberg, 1987.

Juta, Jan. *Look Out for the Ostriches: Tales of South Africa*. Cape Town: CNA Dassie Books, 1949.

Keats, Felicity. *The Wild Swarm*. Cape Town: Tafelberg, 1987.

Kenmuir, Dale. *Dry Bones Rattling*. Pretoria: De Jager-HAUM, 1990.

Kenmuir, Dale. *Ol' Tangletooth*. Pretoria: De Jager-HAUM, 1990.

Kenmuir, Dale. *Song of the Surf*. Cape Town: Maskew Miller Longman, 1988.

Kenmuir, Dale. *The Tusks and the Talisman*. Pretoria: De Jager-HAUM, 1987.

Kipling, Rudyard. *The Jungle Book*. 1894.

Kipling, Rudyard. *The Second Jungle Book*. 1895.

Kirkwood, Mike. 'The colonizer: a critique of the English South African culture theory,' in *Poetry South Africa: Selected Papers from Poetry 74*, ed. P. Wilhelm and J. Polley. Johannesburg: Ad Donker, 1976, 102-133.

Kühne, Klaus. *The Secret of Big Toe Mountain*. Cape Town: Human &

Rousseau, 1987.

Lanham, L.W. 'South African English as an index of social history.' *English Studies in Africa*, 13:1, March 1970, 251-264.

Lanham, L.W. and Macdonald, C.A. *The Standard in South African English and its Social History*. Amsterdam: Groos, 1979.

Larson, C.R. *The Emergence of African Fiction*. Bloomington: Indiana University Press, 1972.

Lau, Brigitte. *Namibia in Jonker Afrikaner's Time*. Windhoek: National Archives, 1987.

Leach, Edmund. *Culture and Communication: The Logic by which Symbols are Connected*. London: Cambridge University Press, 1976.

Le Guin, Ursula. *Earthsea* trilogy: *The Wizard of Earthsea*. Berkeley: Parnassus Press, 1971; *The Tombs of Atuan*. New York: Athenaeum, 1969; *The Farthest Shore*. New York: Athenaeum, 1972.

Lenta, Margaret. 'Black and white women yesterday and today.' *Current Writing*, 3, October, 1991, 161-166.

Le Roux, Marina. 'Jenny Seed lewer een van die beste jeugboeke van die jaar.' *Die Burger*, 19 November 1987, 4.

Leshoai, B.L. *Iso le Nkhono: African Folktales for Children*. Second edition. Braamfontein: Skotaville, 1983.

Lessing, Doris. *Martha Quest*. London: MacGibbon & Kee, 1965.

Lewis, C.S. *The Lion, the Witch and the Wardrobe*. London, 1950.

Lewis-Williams, J.D. *Discovering Southern African Rock Art*. Cape Town: David Phillip, 1990.

Lighton, R. *Out of the Strong: A Bushveld Story*. London: Macmillan, 1957. First published 1956.

Liguori-Reynolds, Rosalie. *Khoko the Lazy*. Johannesburg: Educum, 1981.

Linde, Freda. *The Singing Grass*. London: Oxford University Press, 1975.

Lord, Albert B. *The Singer of Tales*. Cambridge, Mass.: Harvard University Press, 1960.

Louw, Anna. 'The Percy FitzPatrick Award for children's books.' *CRUX*, 11:2, April 1977, 3-10.

Ludman, Barbara. *The Day of the Kugel*. Cape Town: Maskew Miller Longman, 1989.

Mackenzie, John M. *The Empire of Nature: Hunting, Conservation and British Imperialism*. Manchester: Manchester University Press, 1988.

Makhuphula, Nombulelo. *Xhosa Fireside Tales*. Johannesburg: Seriti sa Sechaba, 1988.

Mangan, J.A. *The Games Ethic and Imperialism*. Harmondsworth: Viking, 1986.

Margoles, Mitzi and Hoffenberg, Sheila. *Mandu and the Forest Guard-*

ian. Cape Town: Tafelberg, 1987.

Markowitz, A. *The Rebirth of the Ostrich, and Other Stories of the Kalahari Bushmen Told in their Manner*. Gaborone: National Museum and Art Gallery, 1971.

Markowitz, A. *With Uplifted Tongue: Stories, Myths and Fables of the South African Bushmen told in their Manner*. Cape Town: Central News Agency Limited, 1956.

Martin, M.C. 'Jenny Seed's South African books.' *Libri Natales*, July 1971, 12-14.

Matthee, Dalene. *Fiela's Child*. Harmondsworth: Viking, 1987.

McMagh, Patricia. 'What are we going to teach? And how?' *CRUX*, 4:7, August 1967, 43-47.

Metelerkamp, Sanni. *Outa Karel's Stories: South African Folklore Tales*. London: Macmillan, 1914.

Metrowich, F.C. *The Valiant But Once*. Cape Town: Howard Timmins, 1956.

Meyer, Grace. *Where the Marula Grows*. Johannesburg: Book Studio, 1988.

Mhlophe, Gcina. *The Snake with Seven Heads*. Braamfontein: Skotaville, 1989.

Miller, Penny. *Myths and Legends of Southern Africa*. Cape Town: Bulpin, 1979.

Milne, A.A. *Winnie-the-Pooh*. London: Methuen, 1937. First published 1926.

Molakeng, Tshokolo wa. 'Sangomas who won't give up an ancient power.' *Weekly Mail*, 18 February 1991, 21-22.

Montgomery, L.M. *Anne of Green Gables*. Boston, 1908.

Mphahlele, Es'kia. *Father Come Home*. Johannesburg: Ravan Press, 1984.

Murgatroyd, Madeline. *Maduma, Teller of Tales*. Cape Town: Tafelberg, 1987.

Murgatroyd, Madeline. *Tales from the Kraals*. Cape Town: Howard Timmins, 1968.

Mutwa, Credo Vusamazulu. *Africa is my Witness*. Johannesburg: Blue Crane Books, 1966.

Mutwa, Credo Vusamazulu. *Indaba, my Children*. Johannesburg: Blue Crane Books, 1964.

O'Brien, R.C. *Mrs Frisby and the Rats of NIMH*. Harmondsworth: Puffin, 1975. First published 1971.

Opie, Frank W.J. *The Outdoor Classroom*. Cape Town: Maskew Miller Longman, 1989.

Orwell, George. *Animal Farm*. London: Heinemann Educational Books, 1975. First published, 1945.

Owen, Phyllis. *Out of the Twilight*. Pretoria: Daan Retief, 1989.

Parker, Carolyn. *Witch Woman on the Hogsback*. Pretoria: De Jager-HAUM, 1987.

Parker, Kenneth. 'Imagined revolution: Nadine Gordimer's *A Sport of Nature*,' in *Women and Writing in South Africa: A Critical Anthology*, ed. Cherry Clayton. Johannesburg: Heinemann, 1989, 209-223.

Parkman, Francis. *The Oregon Trail: Sketches of Prairie and Rocky-Mountain Life*. New York: Random House, 1849.

Partridge, A.C. *Folklore of Southern Africa*. Cape Town: Purnell, 1973.

Partridge, A.C., ed. *Readings in South African Prose*. Second and revised edition. Pretoria: J.L. van Schaik Ltd, 1948.

Partridge, A.C., ed. *Scenes from South African Life*. London: Evans Brothers, 1969.

Paton, Jonathan, and Janks, Hillary. 'English and the teaching of English literature in South Africa,' in *Teaching and Learning English Worldwide*, ed. James Britton, Robert E. Shafer and Ken Watson. Clevedon, Philadelphia: Multilingual Matters, 1990, 226-248.

Pearce, Philippa. *Tom's Midnight Garden*. London: Oxford University Press, 1958.

Phillips, Mary. *The Bushman Speaks*. Cape Town: Howard Timmins, 1961.

Phillips, Mary. *The Cave of Uncle Kwa: A Bushman Fantasy*. Cape Town: Purnell, 1965.

Pieterse, Pieter. *The Misty Mountain*. Pretoria: De Jager-HAUM, 1985.

Pitcher, Diana. *The Calabash Child: African Folk-tales adapted and retold*. Cape Town: David Philip, 1980.

Pitcher, Diana. *The Mischief Maker: African Tales of Nogwaja the Hare*. Cape Town: David Philip, 1984.

Player, Ian. 'One earth,' in *Rotating the Cube: Environmental Strategies for the 1990s*, ed. Graham Howe. Durban: Department of Geographical and Environmental Sciences and Indicator Project South Africa, University of Natal, 1990, 5-7.

Plomer, William. *Turbott Wolfe*. London: The Hogarth Press, 1926.

Pohl, Victor. *Bushveld Adventures*. Fifth edition. Johannesburg: APB Publishers, 1970. First published, 1940.

Pohl, Victor. *Farewell, the Little People*. Cape Town: Oxford University Press, 1968.

Pohl, Victor. *Land of Distant Horizons*. Johannesburg: APB Publishers, 1946.

Poland, Marguerite. 'Do local children still believe in pink elephants?' *Sunday Times Magazine*, 14 March 1982, 5.

Poland, Marguerite. *Marcus and the Boxing Gloves*. Cape Town: Tafelberg.

Poland, Marguerite. *Marcus and the Go-kart.* Cape Town: Tafelberg, 1988.

Poland, Marguerite. *Nqalu, the Mouse with No Whiskers.* Cape Town: Tafelberg, 1980.

Poland, Marguerite. *Once at KwaFubesi.* Johannesburg: Ravan Press, 1981.

Poland, Marguerite. *Sambane's Dream and Other Stories.* Harmondsworth: Penguin, 1989.

Poland, Marguerite. *Shadow of the Wild Hare.* Cape Town: David Philip, 1986.

Poland, Marguerite. *The Bush Shrike.* Johannesburg: Ravan Press, 1982.

Poland, Marguerite. *The Mantis and the Moon: Stories for the Children of Africa.* Johannesburg: Ravan Press, 1979.

Poland, Marguerite. *The Small Clay Bull.* Cape Town: David Philip, 1986.

Poland, Marguerite. *The Wood-ash Stars.* Cape Town: David Philip, 1983.

Poland, Marguerite. *Train to Doringbult.* London: Bodley Head, 1987.

Potter, Beatrix. *The Tale of Peter Rabbit.* First published, 1900.

Preston-Whyte, Rob. 'The environmental rubic cube,' in *Rotating the Cube: Environmental Strategies for the 1990s,* ed. Graham Howe. Durban: Department of Geographical and Environmental Sciences and Indicator Project South Africa, University of Natal, 1990, 8-9.

Prestyn-Thomas, Patricia. *Moontide.* Harmondsworth: Puffin, 1987.

Pretoria News. 'Two tales added to animal stories,' review of *Sambane's Dream and Other Stories* by 'S.M.', 29 October 1990.

Prettejohn, Alix. *The Poacher of Hidden Valley.* Pretoria: Daan Retief, 1986.

Rice, M.C. 'From Dolly Gray to Sarie Marais: a survey of fiction in English concerning the First and Second Anglo-Boer conflicts.' Unpublished D Litt et Phil thesis. Johannesburg: Rand Afrikaans University, 1983.

Rive, Richard. 'The black writer and South African literature,' in *Towards Understanding/Op Weg na Begrip,* ed. Isabel Cilliers. Cape Town: Maskew Miller Longman, 1988, 198-209.

Robinson, A.M. Lewin. *None Daring to Make Us Afraid.* Cape Town: Maskew Miller, 1962.

Rosenthal, Eric. *They Walk by Night.* Cape Town: Howard Timmins, 1949.

Rousseau, Leon Gerdener. *Van Hunks and his Pipe: A Traditional Tale of the Cape.* Trans. Nancy Baines. Cape Town: Timmins, 1966.

Sadler, Celia, comp. *Never a Young Man: extracts from the letters and journals of the Rev. W. Shaw.* Cape Town: HAUM, 1967.

Savory, Phyllis. *African Fireside Tales Part 1: Xhosa, Matabele, Batswana.* Cape Town: Howard Timmins, 1982.

Savory, Phyllis. *The Best of African Folklore.* Cape Town: Struik, 1988.

Savory, Phyllis. *The Little Wise One: African Tales of the Hare.* Cape Town: Tafelberg, 1990.

Scheub, Harold. Introduction to *Tales from Southern Africa* by A.C. Jordan. Berkeley: University of California Press, 1973.

Schmidt, Nancy J. 'Jenny Seed,' in *Twentieth Century Children's Writers*, ed. D.L. Kirkpatrick. Second edition. New York: St Martin's Press, 1985, 682-683. Reprinted in *Newsletter of the United States Board on Books for Young People*, Fall 1986, 10.

Schreiner, Olive. *The Story of an African Farm.* 1883.

Seed, Jenny. *Canvas City.* London: Hamish Hamilton, 1968.

Seed, Jenny. *Gold Dust.* London: Hamish Hamilton, 1982.

Seed, Jenny. *Khulumi the Brave.* London: Hamish Hamilton, 1970.

Seed, Jenny. *Place Among the Stones.* Cape Town: Tafelberg, 1987.

Seed, Jenny. *Strangers in the Land.* London: Hamish Hamilton, 1976.

Seed, Jenny. *The Broken Spear.* London: Hamish Hamilton, 1972. Revised edition, Cape Town: Tafelberg, 1988.

Seed, Jenny. *The Bushman's Dream: African Tales of the Creation.* London: Hamish Hamilton, 1975.

Seed, Jenny. *The Far-away Valley.* Pretoria: Daan Retief, 1987.

Seed, Jenny. *The Great Thirst.* London: Hamish Hamilton, 1971. Revised edition, Cape Town: Tafelberg, 1985.

Seed, Jenny. *The New Fire.* Cape Town: Human & Rousseau, 1983.

Seed, Jenny. *The Policeman's Button.* Cape Town: Human & Rousseau, 1981.

Seed, Jenny. *The Prince of the Bay.* London: Hamish Hamilton, 1970.

Seed, Jenny. *The Red Dust Soldiers.* London: William Heinemann, 1972.

Seed, Jenny. *The Spy Hill.* Cape Town: Human & Rousseau, 1984.

Seed, Jenny. *The Unknown Land.* London: William Heinemann, 1976.

Seed, Jenny. *The Voice of the Great Elephant.* London: Hamish Hamilton, 1968.

Seed, Jenny. *The Year One.* London: Hamish Hamilton, 1980.

Seed, Jenny. *Vengeance of the Zulu King.* London: Pantheon, 1971.

Seed, Jenny. *Warriors on the Hills.* London: Abelard Schuman, 1975.

Sendak, Maurice. *Where the Wild Things Are.* New York, 1963.

Slingsby, Peter. *Leopard Boy.* Cape Town: Tafelberg, 1989.

Smedman, M. Sarah. 'Esther Forbes' *Johnny Tremain*: authentic history, classic fiction,' in *Touchstones: Reflections on the Best in Children's Literature*, ed. Perry Nodelman. West Lafayette: Children's Literature Association, 1985, 83-95.

Smith, Janet. *Streams to Rivers.* Cape Town: Maskew Miller Longman,

1988.

Smith, Pauline. *Platkops Children*. First published, 1935.

Smith, Pauline. *The Little Karoo*. London: Cape, 1925.

Stalten, Felix. *Bambi*. First published, 1928.

Star. 16 February 1991, 2; and 6 March 1991, 2.

Stevenson-Hamilton, J. *Animal Life in Africa*. London: Heinemann, 1919.

Stevenson-Hamilton, J. 'Foreword,' in *Our South African National Parks*. Cape Town: United Tobacco Company, 1940, iv-vii.

Stevenson Hamilton, J. *South African Eden*. London: Cassell, 1937.

Stillwell, Valerie. *Monsters, Heroes and Sultans' Daughters: Cape Malay Folk Tales retold*. Cape Town: Human and Rousseau, 1986.

Stokes, C.S. *Sanctuary*. Cape Town: Sanctuary Production Committee, 1942.

Stokes, C.S. *We're Telling You*. Cape Town: Kathhriadon Publications, 1943.

Sunday Times. 17 February 1991, 5.

Sutherland, W.S. *The Horizons of the Hunter*. Pretoria: Daan Retief, 1987.

Thesen, Hjalmar. *A Deadly Presence*. Cape Town: David Philip, 1982.

Thomas, E.W. *Bushman Stories*. Cape Town: Oxford University Press, 1950.

Tötemeyer, Andreé-Jeanne. 'Impact of African mythology on South African juvenile literature.' *South African Journal of Library and Information Science*, 57:4, December 1989, 393-401.

Tötemeyer, Andreé-Jeanne. 'Towards interracial understanding through South African children's and youth literature,' in *Towards Understanding/Op Weg na Begrip: Children's Literature for Southern Africa*, ed. Isabel Cilliers. Cape Town: Maskew Miller Longman, 1988, 80-88.

Tracey, Hugh. *The Lion on the Path and Other African Stories*. London: Routledge and Kegan Paul, 1967.

Trollope, Anthony. *The Small House at Allington*. 1864.

Tucker, John. 'South African novel which never once mentions race.' *Pretoria News*, 7 January 1957.

Turner, Ethel. *Seven Little Australians*. London: Ward Lock, 1894.

United Tobacco Company. *Our South African Birds*. Cape Town, 1941.

United Tobacco Company. *Our South African Flora*. Cape Town, n.d.

United Tobacco Company. *Our South African National Parks*. Cape Town, 1940.

United Tobacco Company. *Our South Africa Past and Present*. Cape Town, 1938.

Uttley, Alison. *How Little Grey Rabbit Got Back her Tail*. London:

Heinemann, 1930. etc.

Van Straten, Cicely. *The Great Snake of Kalungu and Other Adventures.* Johannesburg: Juventus, 1981.

Van Wyk, Chris. *A Message in the Wind.* Cape Town: Maskew Miller Longman, 1982.

Van Wyk Smith, M. *Grounds of Contest.* Cape Town: Juta & Co, 1990.

Vaughan, Iris. *The Diary of Iris Vaughan.* Cape Town: Central News Agency, 1958.

Vilakazi, Herbert. 'Educating for the future,' quoted in *Race Relations News*, Dec. 1987, 16.

Von Wielligh, G.R. *Boesman-stories (Deel 1): Mitologie en Legendes.* Cape Town: Nasionale Pers, 1919.

Wagner, Gillian. *Children of the Empire.* London: Weidenfeld and Nicolson, 1982.

Watson, Lyall. *The Lightning Bird: The Story of One Man's Journey into Africa's Past.* New York: Dulton, 1982.

Watson, Stephen. 'Recent white South African poetry and the language of liberalism,' in *Publisher/Writer/Reader: Sociology of Southern African Literature,* ed. Susan Gardner. Johannesburg: University of the Witwatersrand, 1986, 199-213.

Watts, H.L. 'A social and demographic portrait of English-speaking white South Africans,' in *English-speaking South Africa Today,* ed. André de Villiers. Oxford: Oxford University Press, 1976, 41-89.

White, E.B. *Charlotte's Web.* Harmondsworth: Puffin, 1963. First published, 1952.

Whitwell, Lesley. *Sungura's Tug of War.* Cape Town: Human & Rousseau, 1986.

Whitwell, Lesley. *The Stolen Mealies.* Cape Town: Human & Rousseau, 1989.

Whitwell, Lesley. *Tortoise's Magic.* Cape Town: Human & Rousseau, 1987.

Wilder, Laura Ingalls. *Little House on the Prairie.* New York: Harper, 1935.

Winckler, Heinz. *In the Dead of Night.* Cape Town: Tafelberg, 1984.

Yates, Dornford. *Berry & Co.* London: Ward, Lock & Co., 1951. First published, 1920.

Younghusband, Peter. *Kobie and the Military Road.* Cape Town: Capricorn Publishers, 1987.

Index

C

J

Jock of the Bushveld, see FitzPatrick, Percy
Joelson, Annette, *How the Ostrich got his Name and Other South
   African Stories for Children*, 8
Jones, Toeckey, *Go well, Stay well*, 130, 136-138, 143, 149
Joubert, Elsa, *The Four Friends and Other Tales from Africa*, 17
July's People, see Gordimer, Nadine

K

Keats, Felicity,
   The Wild Swarm, 74, 76, 84
   Die Wilde Swerm, 74
Kenmuir, Dale, 78, 101
   Dry Bones Rattling, 77, 129, 141
   Ol' Tangletooth, 77
   Song of the Surf, 75-76, 99-101
   The Tusks and the Talisman, 77-79, 97, 136
Kgalagadi Tales, see Du Preez, Hanneke
Khoekhoen folktales, *see* Folktales, Khoekhoen
Khoko the Lazy, see Liguori-Reynolds, Rosalie
Khulumi the Brave, see Seed, Jenny
Kipling, Rudyard, *The Jungle Book* stories, 31, 94-95
Kobie and the Military Road, see Younghusband, Peter
Kühne, Klaus, *The Secret of Big Toe Mountain*, 76, 79-80, 83

L

Land of Distant Horizons, see Pohl, Victor
Language, *see* Style, language
Leopard Boy, see Slingsby, Peter
Leshoai, B L, 13
Leshoai, B L, *Iso le Nkhono: African Folktales for Children*, 12, 15-16
Liberal history, *see* Seed, Jenny, historical novels
Lighton, R, *Out of the Strong*, 54
Liguori-Reynolds, Rosalie, 10, 20
   Khoko the Lazy, 18
Linde, Freda, *The Singing Grass*, 99
Literary awards, 4, 27-29, 110-111, 117, 137, 142, 150
Lord of the Flies, see Golding, William
Love, David, see Case, Dianne
Ludman, Barbara, *The Day of the Kugel*, 130, 133, 145, 149

M

Maduma, Teller of Tales, see Murgatroyd, Madeline

Magic in stories, 33, 40

Makhuphula, Nombulelo, 14, 21
  Xhosa Fireside Tales, 10, 12, 20

Mandu and the Forest Guardian, see Margoles, Mitzi and Hoffenberg, Sheila

Manela the Bull Elephant, see Hickey, W A

Manela and the Poachers, see Hickey, W A

Manliness, *see* Characters, male, stereotyped

Marcus and the Boxing Gloves, see Poland, Marguerite

Marcus and the Go-kart, see Poland, Marguerite

Margoles, Mitzi and Hoffenberg, Sheila, *Mandu and the Forest Guardian*, 74, 82

Marivate, C T D, *see* Baumbach, E J M and Marivate, C T D

Markets, *see* Publishing industry in South Africa

Markowitz, A,
  The Rebirth of the Ostrich, 39-40
  With Uplifted Tongue, 39-40

Metelerkamp, Sanni, 22
  Outa Karel's Stories: South African Folklore Tales, 8, 17

Meyer, Grace, *Where the Marula Grows*, 135, 140-142

Mhlophe, Gcina, *The Snake with Seven Heads*, 10, 20

Missionaries, 8, 10, 62, 114

Modern children's literature, *see* Children's literature, on contemporary themes

Modern colloquial language, *see* Style, language

Monsters, Heroes and Sultan's Daughters: Cape Malay Folktales Retold, see Stillwell, Valerie

Moontide, see Prestyn-Thomas, Patricia

Motives and attitudes of writers, *see* Translations of folktales, motives and attitudes of writers

Mowgli, 31, 94-95

Mphahlele, Es'kia, *Father Come Home*, 139, 141

Mrs Frisby and the Rats of NIMH, see O'Brien, R C

Murgatroyd, Madeline, 12, 17, 21
  Maduma, Teller of Tales, 18
  Tales from the Kraals, 12, 14, 17, 34

Mysterious themes in stories, *see* Environmental education through fiction, themes of the mysterious

Mystic-naturalist tradition, *see* Naturalist-mystic tradition

Mystical relationship between humans, animals and the environment, 83, 86-87, 90-91, 93-94, 103-107, 140, 151

quality/standards
Stillwell, Valerie, 17
  Monsters, Heroes and Sultan's Daughters: Cape Malay Folktales Retold, 9-10
Stokes, C S,
  Sanctuary, 55, 70
  We're Telling You, 55-56
Strangers in the Land, see Seed, Jenny
Streams to Rivers, see Smith, Janet
Style, 16, 78, 81, 105-106, 150
  dialogue, 17-18, 40-41
  language, 17-19, 21, 39-40, 75, 82, 90, 135, 148
  narration and narrators, 13, 17, 20-21, 25, 131, 136, 143-144, 150
Style, *see also* under individual authors
Sungura's Tug of War, see Whitwell, Lesley
Sutherland, W S, *The Horizons of the Hunter*, 147-148
Symbolism, *see* Environmental education through fiction, themes of the mysterious

---

T

Tales from the Kraals, see Murgatroyd, Madeline
Tales of the Trickster Boy, see Cope, Jack
Tales of Veld and Vlei: for Junior High Schools, see Coetzer, J P
The Battle of the Mountain, see Chalmers, Judy
The Best of African Folklore, see Savory, Phyllis
The Boy and the Tree, see Brown, Vivienne Johns
The Broken Spear, see Seed, Jenny
The Bush Shrike, see Poland, Marguerite
The Bushman Speaks, see Phillips, Mary
The Bushman's Dream, see Seed, Jenny
The Bushmen and their Stories, see Helfman, Elizabeth
The Calabash Child, see Pitcher, Diana
The Cave of Uncle Kwa: a Bushman fantasy, see Phillips, Mary
The Day of the Kugel, see Ludman, Barbara
The Earth must be Free, see Grobbelaar, Pieter W
The Far-away Valley, see Seed, Jenny
The Four Friends and Other Tales from Africa, see Joubert, Elsa
The Great Hunters, see Haresnape, Geoffrey
The Great Snake of Kalungu and Other Stories, see Van Straten, Cicely
The Great Thirst, see Seed, Jenny
The Horizons of the Hunter, see Sutherland, W S
The Kayaboeties, see Bregin, Elana
The Little Wise One, see Savory, Phyllis

X

Xhosa Fireside Tales, see Makhuphula, Nombulelo
Xironga Folk-tales, see Baumbach, E J M and Marivate C T D

Y

Younghusband, Peter, *Kobie and the Military Road*, 81, 140-141, 148-149